THE GREAT WREATH BOOK

THE GREAT WREATH BOOK

49 Prizewinning Designs from Woman's Day®

THERESA CAPUANA

MEREDITH® PRESS

New York

Credits & Acknowledgments

For Woman's Day®
    Editor-in-Chief, *Woman's Day*: Jane Chesnutt
    Editorial Project Director: Geraldine Rhoads
    Editor: Theresa Capuana
    Illustrator: Roberta Frauwirth
    Photographers: Bradley Olman, Ben Calvo

Meredith® Press is an imprint of Meredith® Books:
    President, Book Group: Joseph J. Ward
    Vice President, Editorial Director: Elizabeth P. Rice

For Meredith® Press:
    Executive Editor: Connie Schrader
    Associate Editor: Carolyn Mitchell
    Project Editor: Bob Oskam
    Production Manager: Bill Rose

Design by Stanley S. Drate, Folio Graphics Co. Inc.;
Linda Vermie and the Meredith Books Art Department

Packaged by Rapid Transcript, a division of March Tenth, Inc.

Distributed by Meredith Corporation
Des Moines, Iowa

ISBN: 0-696-02363-6
Library of Congress Catalog Card Number: 90-064242

Printed in the United States of America
10 9 8 7 6 5 4 3 2

Dear Crafter,

No one can accuse the 49 prizewinners of the Woman's Day–sponsored wreath contest of "resting on their laurels." They helped create a book that is more than a showcase for wreaths—it's a celebration of triumphs! It has been our privilege at Meredith Press to garner all that talent into one project-packed volume.

Wreaths have always symbolized the cycle of life and fertility, and *The Great Wreath Book* echoes the passage of time and traditions. What makes this selection engaging is the sense of continuation, the passing on of creative inspiration. In assembling a wreath, you form an indelible reminder of seasons, holidays, events, and days past. We hope the step-by-step instructions included in this text make that easy to achieve, and that the crafters' stories and special designer tips make it fun.

As in all of the books we offer, each project is accompanied by a gorgeous full-color photograph and a thorough materials list. We also provide a General Directions chapter, which outlines all the skills you'll need, from basic to innovative techniques. Then, the best part of wreath-making—the personal imprint—is entirely up to you!

Sincerely,

The Editors

CONTENTS

Preface

Coast to Coast: A Sense of Place

Bringing in the Garden

With a Thought for Children

Gifts of Love and Friendship

The Keepsake Wreath

Sentimental Journeys to a Gentler Time

Keeping the Christmas Tradition

General Directions

Index

PREFACE

- First graders in Sturgis, South Dakota, know it's "President's Day month" when Dawn Geppert's flag wreath goes up.
- Debbie Damian heralds spring with an Easter Egg wreath.
- An ardent organic gardener, Deborah DeRosa creates a wreath each year to showcase prize blossoms from her backyard garden.
- And Christabel Dawson "cooks up" a Hands and Hearts Christmas wreath for her grandchildren each year.

A wreath can be almost anything you want it to be: It can be romantic, funny, commemorative, or purely decorative—almost anything goes. The forty-nine wreaths in this book were all winners of a *Woman's Day* magazine wreath contest. They were selected from more than four thousand entries.

Every wreath is different: Each was designed with a different purpose and each one tells a story about its designer.

Each wreath-maker has figured out unique working techniques: A letter opener is used to insert fabric into plastic foam; a corsage pin is used to hold delicate ribbon loops in place until glue can dry; pill bottles are the molds for shaping clay flowers.

At least two of the wreath designers wire and sew their wreaths so they can be changed later. Most other designers are devoted to the glue gun—and provide some valuable tips about using it successfully.

Many wreath-makers spray their finished creations to stiffen bows or give body to the flowers they've used, but at least one is opposed to using spray. We cite favorite sprays by name, when this seems useful, though environmental concerns are inspiring manufacturers to bring many new or reformulated sprays to market as we go to press.

Incidentally, a good many of the designers represented here are not trained crafters. One of our wreaths was executed by the designer's high school daughter and her friends, and many represent projects in which children and other family members were helpers.

When you select the wreath you want to make, you'll work step-by-step with the designer's instructions, but you'll also enjoy rambling through the text to pick up other designers' crafting hints. Soon you'll be inspired and want to work on other wreaths.

Wreaths make great gifts. Crafter after crafter introduced in this collection has used a wreath as a special gift. "A wreath is so easy to personalize." Elements in it can be made to match someone's decor; it can include mementoes—pictures, favorite flowers, objects that speak to the hobbies or interests of the recipient.

Another favorite is the keepsake wreath. Like women in an earlier era who stitched snippets of their wedding dress or other memorabilia into the quilts they made, today's wreath-makers seek to capture memories. *The Great Wreath Book* includes a small selection of these tributes. LoRae Pursian's unique wreath displaying her grandmothers' and great grandmothers' sewing notions (page 114) is a prime example of this type of wreath.

More than half of the designers in this book have sold their work. Some happily combine modest home businesses with time spent with their young children; many are in the process of starting their own wreath-making business. Some are at pin-money profit levels, but others have successful full-time businesses. Some of the wreaths we show here are their best-sellers, and their stories often reveal the strategies that have brought them success.

We have also included in *The Great Wreath Book* their techniques for hanging their wreaths, for keeping them fresh, for storing them, for coping with some of the ticklish little problems they encountered, for making some steps go faster.

These original and helpful tips have been augmented with professional know-how from the editor, Theresa Capuana. Terry was for many years the Needlework and Crafts Editor of *Woman's Day*. In that capacity, she brought to her readers crafts projects designed exclusively for her by major crafts artists and fashion designers, discovered new designers among the magazine's readers, and worked with museum curators and others to reproduce ethnic and historic designs in projects for the magazine.

She has served on numerous crafts juries and boards, including New York State Craftsmen and American Craft Enterprises, and writes and designs on her own.

"These wreaths," she says, "are amazing in the way they mirror American life in the nineties. In years previous people like these designers made quilts. Their successors today are hard pressed to find time for all they would like to do, and the few hours required to design and assemble a wreath make this a favorite creative outlet.

"The expression is so personal, so American," Terry says, comparing this collection with wreath designs from other countries. "They touch so many aspects of our lives—our family attachments, a harkening to the past, our interest in the environment and concerns about recycling, a persistent patriotism. The people who made them have a totally free, untrammelled attitude toward celebrating any event or person or place that takes their fancy. They incorporate in their designs everything from valuable and irreplaceable memorabilia, to found objects of no real value whatever. The end results are unique, and striking.

"I find them most inspiring," Terry says, "and am sure they will awaken many readers' creative instincts."

COAST TO COAST:
A SENSE OF PLACE

MONTANA BOUNTY

*Heart-shaped slices from a favorite fruit produce
a wreath of sweet sentiments.*

Jo Forsberg of Ennis, Montana

J o Forsberg grew up in the Brontë country of Yorkshire, England, and after finishing school went to work for a family in Germany. There she met her husband. Several years ago they moved from Minneapolis to the Big Sky country with their two children. The Forsbergs have five apple trees—and use apples for everything.

   Jo has shown her crafts for some years at the local Christmas bazaar, always trying for something out of the ordinary, "so as not to have too much competition." She bombed with some potpourris and sachets, she says, and her best seller was her fruit leather, an apple confection—that is, until she developed her apple wreath.

TO MAKE THE WREATH

1 Spray the dried apple slices twice on both sides with the sealer; let dry thoroughly.

2 Draw a heart 15½ inches wide and 15 inches high on paper (see How to Design Heart Shapes, page 155).

3 To make the heart frame, place the heart pattern on the cardboard and draw around it. Draw a second heart in the center, allowing for a 2-inch border all around. Cut out the heart frame with the knife.

4 To finish the back of the heart frame, place it on the muslin square; hold it in place with masking tape.

5 Trace the heart outlines on the muslin. Add a ¾-inch seam allowance all around, inside and out.

6 Cut along the outside seam allowance; remove the masking tape from the outer edge and make a series of snips along the seam allowance, forming tabs.

7 Pull and turn the tabs to the front of the heart frame and attach them with the glue gun.

8 Follow Steps 6 and 7 for the inner edge of the heart frame.

9 Attach a hanger to the base (see How to Hang Your Wreath, page 149).

10 Working on the front of the cardboard, position the rose leaves randomly along the edges of the frame, allowing them to overhang slightly.

11 Glue the dried apple slices around the heart, slightly overlapping them. Cover any gaps at the top and bottom with more apple slices.

12 Fill spaces with bay leaves, cinnamon sticks, nutmegs, and small clusters of baby's breath, gluing them to hold.

SIZE
Approximately 16½" wide
   × 16" high

BASE
Open cardboard heart
   covered in muslin, 15½"
   wide × 15" high

MATERIALS AND TOOLS
10–12 medium Red
   Delicious apples, cut into
   ¼"-thick slices and dried
   (see How to Dry Apples,
   page 14)
6 whole nutmegs
10–12 cinnamon sticks
14 bay leaves
8 small clusters of baby's
   breath
15 artificial silk rose leaves
Corrugated cardboard
   or foamcore, 16" square
Stiff paper
Transfer paper
Muslin, 18" square
Pencil
Scissors
Utility knife
Masking tape
Glue gun
Clear acrylic gloss spray
   sealer

HOW TO DRY APPLES

1 Cut the unpeeled and uncored apples lengthwise into ¼-inch slices, producing heart-shaped pieces.

2 To prevent discoloration, mix the pint of lemon juice with one tablespoon of salt in the large bowl and soak the slices for three minutes.

3 Place the slices on the dehydrator trays and let dry for six to twelve hours, or until the apples are brittle.

4 If a dehydrator is not available, the apple slices can be dried on shallow wood trays in the oven. These are simple wood frames at least 1½ inches narrower than the inside of the oven. They can be made from artist's canvas stretchers to which you nail ungalvanized screening, mesh with a high melting point, or wood slats spaced from ¼ to ½ inch apart.

5 Place two layers of cheesecloth on each tray to prevent the apples from sticking.

6 Put the trays into a 140° oven for two hours. Prop the door open to allow air to circulate: 8 inches for a gas oven and ½ inch for an electric oven. Increase heat to 160° for two hours, and then reduce the temperature to 140° until the fruit is dry, about five to seven hours in all.

INGREDIENTS AND UTENSILS

10–12 medium Red Delicious apples (do not peel or core them)
1 pint bottle lemon juice
1 tablespoon salt
Sharp kitchen knife
Large bowl, for soaking apple slices
Dehydrator, or see instructions to make an oven drying tray

PIGGIE HEAVEN

A wreath is a splendid vehicle for expressing a creative crafter's major interests, as here, in the imaginative design hanging in the farm home of a specialist in Purebred Registered Yorkshire hogs. But notice also how versatile her design is: She can replace the pigs with white satin hearts for a wedding or with red satin ones for Valentine's Day. A small silk American flag in the bow can celebrate the Fourth of July, or a white satin cross hung in the open center can mark the Easter season.

Yvonne H. Childs of Cairo, Georgia

On approaching the Childs' home, you pass through an iron archway with a cast-iron pig at the top center and below it a sign reading "Hog Heaven." Yvonne worked in television before marrying farmer Elwyn Childs and has worked in public health for the last twenty years. But her spare-time interests focus on the farm.

She says she's always liked pigs, collects pig items of all descriptions, and now has well over 2,000 "of every design you can imagine." She grew up a 4-H'er, has been a volunteer 4-H leader since college, has served in all the officer positions of the State 4-H Volunteer Leader Association, and has for many years sat on the Board of Directors of the organization for all 4-H'ers who have been state winners. (Incidentally, that organization includes all three of the Childs' grown children, one of whom was also a national winner at age thirteen.)

Yvonne designs and sews most of her clothes, also making fabric-covered shoes and jewelry to match. Her Victorian-decorated home accounts for Yvonne's Christmas touches—they're always all white, satin roses with pearls and lace—and, for the year they participated in the Cairo Christmas Tour of Homes, the satin angel pigs seen starring here.

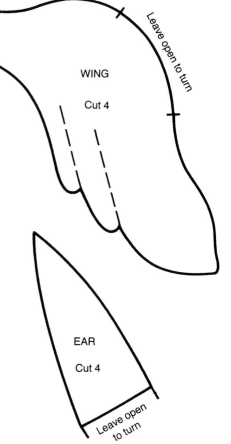

WING

Cut 4

Leave open to turn

EAR

Cut 4

Leave open to turn

TO MAKE THE WREATH

1 To make four satin pigs, trace the pattern parts. Transfer eight bodies, sixteen ears, and sixteen wings to the back of the satin, remembering to flop half of the body and wing patterns needed so the shiny side of the fabric is always on the outside of the pig. Add ⅛-inch seam allowances. Cut out all pieces around seam allowances.

2 Matching fronts to backs of pairs of bodies, ears, and wings, and with the shiny sides facing each other, pin and then stitch around seam allowances, leaving indicated areas open for turning and stuffing.

3 Turn the sewn parts with the right (shiny) side out, and stuff firmly with the fiberfill.

4 Carefully hand-sew all the openings closed, including the bottoms of the ears.

5 Topstitch along dotted lines marked on the wing and body patterns.

6 Follow the pattern markings to position the ears and wings on the bodies; glue to hold.

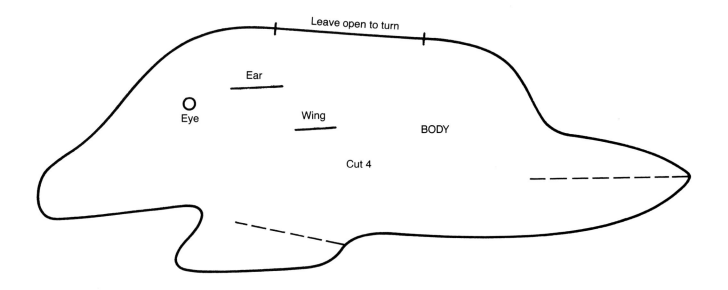

Leave open to turn

Ear

Eye

Wing

BODY

Cut 4

7 Glue a pair of eyes onto each pig where shown.

8 Wind the white ribbon around the wreath, completely covering it. Glue the ends to the wreath.

9 Overwrap the first layer of ribbon with 7 yards of the white lace ribbon, again gluing the ends to the wreath.

10 Attach a hanger to the base (see How to Hang Your Wreath, page 149).

11 Position the roses, rosebuds, and jasmine blossoms around the wreath as shown in the photograph. Attach them one by one with a glue gun.

12 Glue the rose-leaf clusters here and there around the wreath.

13 Evenly space the lily-of-the-valley sprays around the wreath and glue.

14 Wrap the satin cord once around the wreath, using floral U-pins to hold it in place. Repeating the same technique, wrap the pearl roping twice.

15 With 4¼ yards of the lace ribbon, form a bow with seventeen 4½-inch loops (see To Form a Florist's Bow, page 154).

16 Cut 8- and 24-inch lengths from the remaining lace ribbon for streamers.

17 Attach a wire to the end of the 8-inch streamer and one to the center of the 24-inch streamer, and wire them to the back of the bow, letting the ends hang down. Notch the ends.

18 Glue the bow and streamers to the top of the wreath.

19 Glue the satin pigs to the wreath, as shown in the photograph.

SIZE
Approximately 22" diameter

BASE
20"-diameter straw wreath

MATERIALS AND TOOLS
½ yard white satin fabric, 45" wide
7 yards white acetate satin ribbon, 2" wide
12½ yards white lace ribbon, 2¼" wide
5' white satin cord
10' pearl roping
Artificial silk flowers and leaves: 43 mixed large and medium white roses and rosebuds; 9 clusters of 5 white jasmine blossoms; 13 clusters of 3 lily-of-the-valley sprays; 29 clusters of 5 rose leaves
8 doll eyes, ⅛" diameter
Fiberfill
White sewing thread and needle
Straight pins
Tracing paper
Transfer paper
Pencil
Scissors
Floral wire
Floral U-pins
Wire cutters
Glue gun

CHILI LIGHTS

The wreath commemorates a visit to Santa Fe. The little church at the bottom represents all the churches and missions around Santa Fe, but particularly the church near the famous square. The cactus to its right represents the high-altitude desert terrain; the pine sprig evokes the chilly temperatures and the famous piñon pines. It's all put together without glue so the materials can be used again, if desired.

Susan Wilson of Lakewood, Colorado

A pine-bough wreath made when she was in the Girl Scouts introduced Susan Wilson to wreath-making. This is her third wreath project, made when she was changing her decor from "primitive" country to Southwestern country. She had collected her ornaments over a period of time and wanted something with lights—with a "festive patio spirit." She enjoys working in watercolors, has a degree in mathematics, and is a computer consultant.

TO MAKE THE WREATH

1   Attach a hanger to the base (see How to Hang Your Wreath, page 149).

2   Attach the battery case to the bottom front of the wreath by wrapping it twice with masking tape.

3   Cut the blue craft ribbon in half; wind it around the battery case and the wreath to cover the masking tape; overlap the ends in back and hand-sew to hold.

4   Place the wreath face up on a flat surface and arrange the lights evenly around. Tape to hold.

5   Tightly wind the rust craft ribbon around the wreath, to hide most of the light cord; adjust the lights so they do not get buried underneath the ribbon.

6   Hand-sew the ribbon ends together in the back.

7   Cut satin ribbon into 12-inch lengths and use to tie on the ornaments—cactus, pine, pinecones, and berries—and also as decoration. Use the crochet hook to pull the ribbons through the strands of willow. Tie them into knots, leaving the ends dangling to resemble pine needles.

8   Make a ring of masking tape with the sticky side out, to attach the church to the battery case.

SIZE
Approximately 18" diameter

BASE
18"-diameter bleached
willow wreath

MATERIALS AND TOOLS
Tree lights with battery pack
Chili tree-light covers
Craft ribbon with
Southwestern motifs, 1⅜"
wide: ¾ yard blue; 7
yards rust
4½ yards grass-green satin
ribbon, ⅛" wide
Southwestern terra cotta
ornaments, at least 5,
approximately 2" high
Stuffed fabric cactus,
approximately 5" high
Artificial pine cluster
3 small pinecones
2 bunches of small, artificial
red berries
Needle and thread
Scissors
Masking tape
Medium crochet hook

ROMANTICIZING THE SCALLOP

Combine roses and shells and satin ribbons and ivy leaves, and you have a wreath that is the ultimate in romantic Victorian feeling. It was made for the designer's bedroom.

Dolores Noel of Vernon, Texas

Dolores Noel wears many hats. Mornings, she babysits for a one-year-old. Afternoons, she works at a gift shop or helps her husband in his John Deere dealership. She also bakes specialty cakes and breads that she sells locally.

Married to her high school sweetheart, she has two sons now winding up their school years.

Dee has no formal training in crafts: "I basically taught myself." Not content with just producing wreaths for sale in the gift shop, she persistently experiments. With a friend, she covered the lattice ceiling of a garden room with artificial silk ivy and various flowers, then added a large swag filled with twigs, flowers, and berries, and added ribbon down one side.

What did she do with the leftover flowers? She made herself a spray to go over her bed, set on a four-foot base, with branches of tulips, roses, iris, dogwood, berries, lilacs, and Queen Anne's lace rising from it.

TO MAKE THE WREATH

1 Attach a hanger to the base (see How to Hang Your Wreath, page 149).

2 Arrange the ivy leaves around the wreath. Pick them up one by one and glue them in place.

3 Position the scallop shells, clustering them here and there, leaving space for the bow. Then glue in place.

4 Arrange the smaller shells on top of the scallop shells and also scatter them around the wreath; glue.

5 Position the peach blossoms and glue to hold.

6 Do the same with the buds and the tiny leaves.

7 From 1 yard of coral ribbon, form a bow with four loops each 3½ inches. Repeat Steps 1 and 2 of To Form a Florist's Bow, page 154, until four loops are formed. Twist wire around middle to hold.

8 Cut a 24-inch length from the remaining coral ribbon for streamers.

9 Center and wire this ribbon to the back of the bow so the two ends hang down as streamers.

SIZE
Approximately 14" diameter

BASE
12"-diameter whitewashed grapevine wreath

MATERIALS AND TOOLS
10 scallop shells, approximately 2" wide
16–20 exotic shells, such as tritons and turbans
Artificial silk flowers and leaves: 13–15 ivy leaves; 17 peach blossoms; 6–8 buds and tiny leaves
Picot-edge satin ribbon, ¼" wide: 1¾ yards coral; 3¾ yards peach; 4½ yards light pink
Glue gun

10 Cut a 1-yard length from both peach and light pink ribbons.

11 Treating them as one, follow Step 7 above to form a bow from these ribbons.

12 Cut 24-inch lengths from the peach and light pink ribbons.

13 Follow Step 9 above to attach streamers to bow.

14 Glue the two bows together. Tie a 25-inch length of light pink ribbon around the middle of the loops, allowing the streamers to hang.

15 Form a loose knot at the end of each streamer.

16 Twist and swirl the remaining 2 yards of the peach and light pink ribbons around the wreath and glue wherever they touch the vine.

17 Glue the bow to the upper left of the wreath, allowing all the streamers to hang.

NOSTALGIA FOR NEW MEXICO

Buffalo gourds from New Mexico roadsides, dried and then painted by the gifted artist and combined with other desert naturals, make this our third-prize winner. It evokes a great sense of place.

Lona Utrup of La Plata, New Mexico

Lona Utrup's work is steeped in the Indian lore of the Southwest. Her favorite designs are the animal figures (*mimbres*) popular on the Acoma pottery and Hopi jewelry common to the region. Traditional Indian colors of black, white, blue, and terra cotta represent earth, clouds, and sun, and fine lines on the designs represent rain.

For several years Lona shipped her painted gourds, charming as Christmas ornaments, to galleries and shops in several states. When she incorporated them into wreaths, she found a ready market for those, too.

Because they now sell so well, she says, "Gathering weeds and seeds has become a family activity."

"When my husband, Mark, four children, and I relocated to La Plata, my husband talked about clearing the land, while I walked behind him, saying, 'Look at all those great weeds!' "

Her enthusiasm for "those weeds" has inspired a new home-based business she calls The Nature of Art. "Having been an art major in college, I now believe some of the most beautiful art forms and designs come from nature itself."

MIMBRES FIGURES

TO MAKE THE WREATH

1 If the straw wreath is covered with plastic, remove the plastic wrapping.

2 Attach a hanger to the base (see How to Hang Your Wreath, page 149).

3 Trace the *mimbres* designs from the patterns and transfer them to the gourds.

4 Paint the gourds, following the photograph for colors.

5 If desired, glue a turquoise stone to each gourd.

6 Wire the 3-inch pinecones around the inner and outer perimeters of the wreath. Use the glue gun for additional hold, if necessary.

7 Position and then hot-glue the gourds around the wreath.

8 Arrange the pods, weeds, and pinecones around the gourds and glue them to hold.

9 Apply several light coats of the sealer to give the wreath a glossy sheen.

10 Glue clusters of baby's breath here and there around the wreath.

11 Finally, glue the pheasant feathers into the wreath, starting on the outside edges and working around the wreath toward the center.

Designer's Note

Not all of Lona Utrup's materials come from New Mexico. Her father sends her the pinecones and pheasant feathers from South Dakota, and she finds the curved weed cat claw in Tucson, Arizona, when she visits there.

She suggests bleaching yucca pods if they are too dark: Put pods into a bucket of water with some bleach to lighten them. Remove the pods and let them dry before working with them.

As for the clear spray sealer, she finds the K-Mart and Wal-Mart brands the best because they do not yellow. She recommends using the sealer before attaching the feathers, to prevent them from matting.

SIZE
Approximately 16" diameter

BASE
14"-diameter straw wreath

MATERIALS AND TOOLS
6 dried buffalo gourds
Approximately 100 pinecones ranging from ½" long to under 3" long
30 pinecones 3" long
Seed pods and desert weeds, such as milkweed, yucca, teasel, and cat claw
Pheasant feathers
6 turquoise stones, no larger than ¾" (optional)
Baby's breath clusters
Tracing paper
Transfer paper
Pencil
Acrylic paints: black, white, terra cotta, and royal blue
Artist's brush
Floral wire
Wire cutters
Glue gun
Clear acrylic gloss spray sealer

MIMBRES FIGURES

TWO HEARTS TOGETHER

This stunning design presents a symmetrical arrangement of pinecones on two heart-shaped bases.

Jaynis Pixley of Newtown, Connecticut

Jaynis Pixley, the thirty-nine-year-old mother of five children ranging in age from four to eleven, describes herself as "a manufacturing engineer turned stay-at-home Mom." She continues, "I teach Sunday school and do crafts projects with two Brownie troops. I also enjoy woodworking, cooking, crocheting, painting, and quilt-making.

"I cannot remember when I wasn't crafts-oriented. My mother recently unearthed something that I had made out of buttons and fabric scraps when I was three years old."

This pinecone heart wreath is a larger version of some she had designed and made to sell at her church Christmas fair.

TO MAKE THE WREATH

1 Draw two hearts on paper, one 23½ inches wide by 20 inches high, and another 12½ inches wide by 9 inches high (see How to Design Heart Shapes, page 155).

2 To make the heart frame, place the large heart pattern on the wood paneling and draw around it. Draw a second heart in the center of this first one, allowing a 3-inch border between the hearts.

3 For the heart that will hang in the middle of the wreath, place the smaller heart pattern in the center of the panel on which you are working, and draw around it.

4 Cut out the heart shapes with a jigsaw, producing the frame and the center heart (see Materials and Tools, page 148). If necessary, smooth all edges with sandpaper.

5 The placement of the pinecones is crucial for achieving the symmetry of this wreath. So first place the long cones in position on both hearts, as shown in the photograph. Then attach them one by one, using a glue gun. Repeat the procedure with the large cones, and then the medium ones.

6 Finally, fill in the heart frame with small cones. Accent both hearts with the sweet gum balls, as shown in the photograph.

SIZE
Approximately 24" wide × 20" high

BASE
Two wood paneling or Masonite hearts: a 23½"-wide × 20"-high open-heart frame and a 12½"-wide × 9"-high center heart

7 Once the pinecones are glued in place, fill in all the edges with scales cut from large cones, using garden shears. Hot-glue these scales in place.

8 Finish by giving the wreath two or three light but thorough coats of polyurethane spray on the front, back, and sides.

9 To join the hearts, turn them over and position the smaller one in the center opening. Glue the ends of an 8-inch length of ribbon to the backs of both hearts as shown in the photograph. Make a bow from a 30-inch length of ribbon, cutting a notch in each end (see To Form a Two-Loop Bow, page 152).

10 Make a hanging loop by gluing the ends of a 16-inch length of ribbon to the back of the large heart.

Designer's Note
The finishing spray enables you to blow the dust off by reversing the suction on your vacuum cleaner.

MATERIALS AND TOOLS

Piece of wood paneling or
    Masonite 24″ square
Pinecones: 10 long,
    11 large, 15 medium, 14
    small
26 sweet gum balls
1½ yards red satin ribbon,
    ⅞″ wide
Ruler
Pencil
Scissors
Garden shears
Medium sandpaper
Stiff paper for patterns
Drill
Jigsaw
Glue gun
Satin polyurethane spray
    varnish

SHELLS FROM SOUTHERN SEAS

This beautifully controlled assembly of seashells, lacquered so they glisten as they might with sea water still on them, is a vivid reminder of sunny times at the beach.

Marjorie Burnett of Marietta, Georgia

Marjorie Burnett is an ardent shell-collector, so after her sister made her a shell wreath, Marjorie promptly made twelve more as presents for friends and relatives.

She is the wife of a scientist, with two married daughters, two granddaughters, and two grandsons. She does landscape painting, crochets lace for linens, loves bridge, camping, and canoeing, and does volunteer work for Americans for International Aid and Adoption.

TO MAKE THE WREATH

1 If the straw wreath is covered with plastic, remove the plastic wrapping.

2 Attach a hanger to the base (see How to Hang Your Wreath, page 149).

3 Place the wreath on a flat work surface with the back facing up. Position a row of clamshells around the outer rim of the wreath, fitting them very snugly next to each other and with the hinge ends facing the front of the wreath. Use the glue gun to attach them one by one.

4 Arrange and glue a tight row of scallop shells on the inner rim of the wreath, with their hinge ends facing the back of the wreath. There will be only about 1¾ inches of straw showing on the back between the clam- and scallop shells.

5 Turn the wreath over and start working on the front. Arrange and glue the largest shells in an attractive design.

6 Add the medium and small shells, paying attention to color and shape and overlapping them where necessary. Completely cover the straw with shells.

7 Finish the design by gluing a starfish-mounted scallop shell to the bottom front of the wreath.

8 Give the wreath two coats of lacquer spray.

SIZE
Approximately 13" diameter

BASE
12"-diameter straw wreath

MATERIALS AND TOOLS
Assortment of exotic seashells, such as conchs, cockles, cowries, tritons, star shells, sea snails
Approximately 14 white clamshells, 2½" wide
Approximately 14 medium scallop shells
1 large scallop shell
1 starfish
Glue gun
Clear high gloss lacquer spray

CRANBERRY JEWEL

This glistening wreath says Welcome: Come in and enjoy our hospitality. *It's perfect for the front door or on windows facing the street.*

Maurice A. Parkonen, Jr., of West Wareham, Massachusetts

Maurice Parkonen has been a professional florist for over twenty-five years, in the course of which he started making his Cranberry Jewel wreath for an Ocean Spray promotion. So many people fell in love with it that he started selling it to order. It is especially popular at Christmas and is perfect as a cold weather outdoor wreath. Warm air, indoors or out, causes the cranberries to dry up and shrink and the greens to shrivel, Maurice notes. "But kept in cool air, it can last for six months."

TO MAKE THE WREATH

1 Attach a hanger to the base (see How to Hang Your Wreath, page 149).

2 Cut the boxwood into two small sprigs; push these pieces into the lower half of the wreath, filling the top and side surfaces until the plastic foam is no longer visible.

3 Using scissors or garden shears, cut the toothpicks in half.

4 Push a half-toothpick into a cranberry, and then push the cranberry into the wreath. (**Note:** Partially freezing the cranberries first and using a thin skewer to make a hole in the plastic foam allows the berry to be handled without being crushed.) Place each cranberry very close to the next until the wreath is totally covered.

5 From 3⅛ yards of the flocked ribbon, form a bow with twelve 4½-inch loops (see To Form a Florist's Bow, page 154).

6 Cut a 12-inch length from the remaining ribbon for streamers. Center and wire the streamers to the back of the bow so the ends hang down, and then wire the bow to the bottom center of the wreath. Cut an inverted notch on each end of the streamers.

Designer's Note

For indoor use or for warm climates, artificial greens might be substituted for the boxwood, and red wooden beads, held with pins or thin nails, could act as a permanent stand-in for the cranberries.

SIZE
Approximately 16" diameter

BASE
14"-diameter green plastic–
foam wreath form

MATERIALS AND TOOLS
One 12-ounce bag
cranberries
Small bunches of boxwood
3¾ yards red flocked
ribbon, 2¾" wide
Round wood toothpicks
Floral preservative spray
Garden shears
Scissors
Thin skewer
Floral wire
Wire cutters

PERENNIAL GARDEN

This conversation piece, painted pinecones wired to a frame, makes a beautiful wall hanging or graces any table. The flowers truly look real and offer a unique way to enjoy summer in winter.

Marjy Sessions of Norway, Maine

Although Marjy Sessions has made twenty or more cone wreaths for her family and friends, this was only her second painted one, and she felt a little guilty, she says, "for gilding the lily."

Marjy's perennials garden and border of flowering shrubs is her favorite hobby, so her floral theme is a natural.

The wreath took most of her spare time for the whole month of January, "a most enjoyable way to spend a cold Maine winter."

She and her husband, both now retired, are busy with the local historical society and veterans' organizations. In fact, they took part in the services in Normandy, France, commemorating the forty-fifth anniversary of the D-day landings of World War II.

With their sons they own and operate a mini-storage facility, and with their families close by, they are able to enjoy six grandchildren—regularly!

TO MAKE THE WREATH

1 Pull damp pliable white cones through the wire frame, alternating the directions of the tops and bottoms as you go; push them as close together as possible. (**Note:** Damp pinecones close up and fit better between the top and bottom wires of the frame, so wet your cones first if they are dry.)

2 Arrange the pinecone-filled frame on a piece of aluminum foil and place into a 200° oven to dry slowly. (**Note:** Use caution, because pinecones are very flammable. It is essential to keep the oven temperature low.)

3 Once the cones are dry, attach a hanger to the base (see How to Hang Your Wreath, page 149).

4 With the shears, cut the rest of the pinecones apart, shredding or even fraying them. Make a rough estimate of the number of pinecones you need by arranging them in a circle the size of the frame.

5 Using the flat dish as a palette, mix small batches of acrylic paints. Primary colors plus white will produce many shades of flower colors.

SIZE
Approximately 18″ diameter

BASE
14″-diameter double wire wreath form

MATERIALS AND TOOLS
28 white pinecones, approximately 5″–6″ long
Approximately 36 small to medium pinecones, such as fir, spruce, hemlock, or Norway pine
Acrylic paints: primary colors, plus white
Medium artist's brush
Flat dish
Aluminum foil
Garden shears
Spool of 30-gauge wire
Wire cutters
Needlenose pliers
Latch hook
Satin polyurethane spray varnish

6 Paint the cut pinecones to resemble garden flowers; let dry.

7 Cut the wire into 8 to 10-inch lengths (as many lengths as you have cones) and wrap around the bottoms of the flower look-alikes.

8 Use the latch hook and needlenose pliers to pull the wires through and twist them to attach the "flowers" to the wire frame, pulling them snug to the base and each other, to prevent them from loosening up later. Because it is very difficult to fill in spaces later without loosening previously attached flowers, fill in as you go, cutting and painting more pinecones as needed.

9 Finish by giving the wreath two or three light but thorough coats of polyurethane spray on the front, back, and sides.

Designer's Note

"Filling the wreath form with white pinecones is the really messy part, as there is no way to avoid getting pitch on your hands. My answer is a hand cleaner that mechanics use.

"Painting the pinecones to look like flowers is the fun part. I paint many more than I think I will need, in case I decide to use more of a different kind or color."

BRINGING IN THE
GARDEN

RING OF ROSES

The spirit of spring itself is captured for all seasons in this arrangement of roses. The designer's use of a porcelain finish produces a look of perennial freshness, and her wreath is a beautiful example of the porcelain technique. Although the wreath looks complicated, it is not all that demanding.

Bobbie Andrews is a musician: She sings, plays the piano and the flute, and gives music lessons at home. She started making wreaths when she didn't find what she wanted at crafts shows. Now, with her sister-in-law, she puts on an annual country Christmas boutique, with about twenty contributing crafters. She loves homemaking, gardening, cooking, and working in her church, and allows six to seven months to prepare for each year's boutique.

Bobbie Eileen Andrews of Englewood, Colorado

SIZE
Approximately 17" diameter

BASE
14"-diameter plastic-foam
wreath

MATERIALS AND TOOLS
Artificial silk flowers and
   leaves in pale colors:
   roses, 3, each
   approximately 4"
   diameter; 25, each 2½"
   diameter; 16, each
   1½" diameter; rosebuds,
   25, each 1¼" diameter;
   18, each 1" diameter
3½ yards pale-blue satin
   ribbon, ¾" wide
16 ounces (one jar) Petal
   Porcelain by Plaid
   Enterprises
Folk Art matte finish spray
   paint, tapioca
Liquid acrylic paints: Cream
   Coat brand in flesh, tan,
   parchment, palomino,
   Wedgwood green, black,
   ripe avocado, bonnie
   blue, dusty mauve;
   Accent Country Colors
   brand in Bordeaux
Brushes: #5 round, #10 flat
Flat dish
Bowl
Newspaper
Cardboard box, slightly
   smaller than wreath
Aluminum foil
Wire cutters
Scissors
Folk Art Clearcote Extra
   Glaze spray

TO MAKE THE WREATH

1 Attach a hanger to the base (see How to Hang Your Wreath,
page 149).

2 Cut the leaves off all the roses with the wire cutters. Put them
aside. Cut the rose stems down to 3 or 4 inches.

3 Insert roses into the wreath form. Start by visualizing a focal
point and cluster the three large roses there. Gradually taper off
around the wreath with the smaller roses and leaves, cutting
stems shorter where necessary. Since the flowers are to be coated,
the color arrangement is not important.

4 Pour the jar of Petal Porcelain into a bowl. Remove flowers
and leaves from the base one by one, and either dip each into the
solution or brush with the porcelain finish. Remove the excess by
turning the flower or leaf upside down and pulling it between
your fingers.

5 As each flower or leaf is completed, replace it on the wreath.

6 Cut ribbon into four pieces, two 38-inch lengths and two 18-inch lengths. Cut inverted notches into the ends.

7 From each of the 38-inch ribbons, form a bow with three 3½-inch loops and two 6-inch streamers. (See To Form a French Bow, page 154. However, follow only Steps 1, 2, and 3 for the French Bow until two loops are formed on one side and only one on the other.) Dip the streamers into the Petal Porcelain and wipe off the excess.

8 Nestle the bows near the three large roses and trail the streamers through the wreath.

9 Brush the loops with Petal Porcelain. Fill the loop openings with crumpled aluminum foil to keep them open and shaped while drying.

10 Dip the remaining two 18-inch ribbon lengths into the Petal Porcelain; remove the excess and then arrange the ribbon between the roses as shown in the photograph.

11 After the wreath is completely filled in, set it on top of an open box with newspaper below to catch the drips.

12 Check for obvious drips, which can be smoothed out by hand or with a brush.

13 After six to eight hours, when the wreath is completely dry, remove the foil supports from the loops. Hold it up to see if there are any empty areas. Correct them by filling in with more roses and leaves, dipping them into the Petal Porcelain and allowing them to dry as before.

14 Give the wreath several light coats of the tapioca matte spray until it is completely covered. Let dry.

15 Shade the roses, leaves, and ribbon by brushing them with the acrylic paints, allowing the tapioca spray undercoat to show through. The flowers are simply tipped in pink tones, the leaves are shaded with avocado and deep rose, and the ribbons are a soft shade of blue. To achieve the pink and deep rose, mix Bordeaux or dusty mauve with the parchment or flesh paints.

16 Spray the wreath with two coats of glaze. Let dry.

Designer's Note
Petal Porcelain is a solution that gives artificial silk flowers a look of porcelain. When working with it, wear an apron to catch the drips, and have a damp cloth handy to wipe fingers clean.

EVERLASTING SPRING

This beautifully composed wreath is distinguished by a lavish use of flowers. Both rich and dense, it is fascinating to explore.

Kathryn D. Fix of Chino Hills, California

Kathryn was introduced to wreath-making by her sister, Sharon Early, of Edmonds, Washington. The inspiration for Kathryn's winning wreath, she says, was "nature." She wanted a vivid display of spring flowers to last through the winter.

Kathryn has been married for thirty years and has five children. She enjoys mountain biking, hiking, and reading. She has been involved in social service work for several years and occasionally speaks before local groups and at local colleges.

TO MAKE THE WREATH

1 For the base, fill the wire wreath form with sheet moss until it is full and round. Wrap floral wire around twice to secure the moss. Use floral U-pins for additional security. Because all the flowers are attached to the moss, the moss should be firmly embedded in the form.

2 Turn the wreath over and attach a hanger to the base (see How to Hang Your Wreath, page 149).

3 Prepare the flowers by shortening the stems.

4 To compose the wreath, begin by spacing four or five pairs of small clusters of fuchsia and purple statice at intervals around the wreath. For the best look, place one of each pair on the inner edge and the other on the outer edge of the wreath. (**Note:** Covering the sides makes a fuller wreath.) Glue to hold.

5 Place roses on the top and sides in small clusters. Attach firmly with a glue gun. Add strawflowers, yarrow, and clusters of hydrangea blossoms to build depth.

6 Finish the wreath by detailing with buds, berries, and leaves. These added touches enhance the wreath.

7 Spray with sealer to protect the flowers.

Designer's Note

"This wreath can last for years," says Kathryn, "if not placed in direct sunlight. I use a small dry paint brush to dust it every few months.

"Before building the wreath, I choose the flowers and greens, separating them and placing them in transparent bags, then use a shoe box to file the bags. This eliminates crushing or digging for flowers and keeps my work area neat."

SIZE
Approximately 16″ diameter

BASE
14″-diameter double wire
   wreath form

MATERIALS AND TOOLS
Sheet moss
Air-dried flowers (see How to
   Dry Flowers and Other
   Naturals, page 157):
   colored statice, yellow
   yarrow, strawflowers,
   delphiniums, carnations
   and buds, bougainvillea,
   rose leaves, elderberries
   or chokeberries
Silica-gel dried flowers (see
   How to Dry Flowers and
   Other Naturals, page
   158): roses and
   buds, hydrangeas
   separated into small
   clusters
Floral U-pins
Floral wire
Scissors or garden shears
Glue gun
Super Surface Sealer from
   Design Master

GARDEN CORNUCOPIA

The showy use of dusty miller and strawflowers in white, pink, and salmon gives this wreath a unique aura. Each year this designer makes a new wreath from her garden flowers so she can enjoy each year's blooms all winter long.

TO MAKE THE WREATH

1 Weave the fresh pliable wisteria vine into an 18-inch diameter wreath, attaching ends with twists of wire. Let it dry, at least overnight.

2 Attach a hanger to the base (see How to Hang Your Wreath, page 149).

3 Completely cover the top and sides of the wreath with Spanish moss; attach it to the vine with the glue gun.

4 Working counterclockwise, glue on fanned-out clusters of dusty miller so all the Spanish moss is covered, including that on the inner and outer edges.

5 Position the strawflowers around the wreath, cutting off the stems if necessary, and then glue them on one by one.

6 Place the rest of the flowers around the wreath until it is entirely covered, again cutting the stems first if necessary. Glue the flowers in place.

7 Fill out with the nigella seed pods. Glue to hold.

8 Spray the wreath with the sealer to help prevent the flowers from shattering.

SIZE
Approximately 19" diameter

BASE
18"-diameter wisteria vine
  wreath

MATERIALS AND TOOLS
Fresh wisteria vine,
  grapevine, or willow
  branches
Spanish moss
Dusty miller
Nigella seed pods
Dried naturals (see How to
  Dry Flowers and Other
  Naturals, page 157):
  white and lavender
  common immortelle;
  white, pink, and blue
  larkspur; white, pink, and
  salmon strawflowers;
  small red and pink roses;
  white winged everlasting;
  pink globe amaranth;
  delphinium florets;
  cockscomb; rose
  everlasting; tansy;
  bachelor buttons;
  quaking grass
Purchased: pink pepper
  berries, preserved cedar
Floral wire
Scissors or garden shears
Wire cutters
Glue gun
Super Surface Sealer from
  Design Master

Deborah DeRosa of Oakdale, New York

Deborah DeRosa became interested in dried flowers and gardening ten years ago, when she quit her job to raise her daughter Lu-Ann Iris (followed two and a half years later by Ivy). She and husband, Dennis, and the girls all garden. She grows everything organically, from seed, "with the help of my praying mantis, bees, butterflies, and good compost."

SHINING WELCOME

Here is a glorious way to capture the beauty of favorite flowers in a wreath that will stay as lovely as ever through many long winters. It offers a wreath-maker many challenges; it is also an opportunity, and an enjoyable one, to play with clay in a most creative way.

Ellen Jane Ferrell of Rockport, Texas

This wreath was inspired by a lovely rose Ellen Jane Ferrell's neighbor brought her from his garden. "I wanted to keep the rose forever," she says, and when a ceramics-designer suggested that she sculpt the rose's twin in low-fired clay, she was so pleased with her results that she began to sculpt other flowers.

She is not a newcomer to crafts. Her earliest creative teaching adventure consisted of decorating mud cakes with toothpaste for her friends, using the techniques she learned from her parents, who owned and operated several bakeries.

At twenty-four, with three young daughters, she found it necessary to augment the family income to enable her husband to attend college. So she baked and decorated wedding cakes and painted plates to sell at the local gift shop.

She is now married to a "mechanical genius" who also loves arts and crafts and also has three daughters. With their six daughters and their families, the Ferrells search for new Christmas ideas all year long and have made many ceramic flower wreaths.

TO MAKE THE WREATH

1 Attach a hanger to the base (see How to Hang Your Wreath, page 149).

2 Cover the work surface with a large piece of plastic, such as a shower curtain or dropcloth. Tape it down.

3 Transfer the flower and leaf patterns to the cardboard and cut out. With these, and cookie cutters (especially circle and scallop-edge shapes in different sizes), you can create many different flowers.

4 Read the directions on the box containing the clay; follow those instructions in processing the clay you have chosen.

5 Take a ball of clay the size of a fist and, using a rolling pin, roll it out until it is the thickness of thin piecrust.

6 Lay the cardboard pattern on the clay and with a sharp paring knife cut around it. Repeat this, as well as cutting shapes with

SIZE
Approximately 17″ diameter

BASE
15″-diameter grapevine wreath sprayed white

MATERIALS AND TOOLS
Air- or oven-drying modeling clay (Sculpey or Della Robbia brands are recommended), 1 box

6 small triton shells (for rosebuds)

For sculpting: rolling pin; nut pick; bamboo sticks; garlic press; paring knife; manicuring orange sticks; flower shape, round, and scalloped-edge cookie cutters; baking pans (if clay is oven-drying)

For drying clay pieces: glass votive candleholders, empty bathroom tissue rolls, used pill vials, aluminum foil

White latex house paint

Liquid acrylic paints in flower and leaf colors and pearlized white for the ribbons

Artist's brush

Thin cardboard

Sandpaper

Ruler

Floral wire

Wire cutters

Scissors

Glue gun and woodworking glue sticks

Clear high-gloss lacquer spray

cookie cutters, until you have approximately thirty flowers of various types and twenty-eight leaves.

7 Gently lift each flower from the rolled-out clay, using the paring knife. Lay it on the end of a cut-down bathroom tissue roll, glass votive candleholder, or pill bottle or other similar holder turned upside down. The clay shape will drape down the sides; at this stage, bend the petals to the flower shapes desired. Do this for every flower, and let air-dry.

8 Remove the leaves from the rolled-out clay and lay them out on a flat surface to dry. Turn them over midway into the drying.

9 For shaping the roses, refer to the Bread Dough Rose directions (Steps 3 through 14) in Roses and Ribbons (pages 62-64). Because the roses on this wreath are bigger, start with a ¾-inch ball of clay for each petal. Roll it out into a round, rather than pressing it between the fingers. Follow the rest of the steps to finish forming the rose. Make two roses, and let them air-dry.

10 Form a baby's breath cluster by rolling a small piece of clay into a 1½-inch ball. Flatten one side. On the rounded side, push in twenty 1¾-inch lengths of wire. Roll out twenty tiny balls of clay, each smaller than a pea, and stick one on the end of each wire. Make six clusters in this fashion. Let air-dry.

11 For a rosebud, partially push a 4-inch length of wire into one end of a triton shell to form a stem. Wrap clay around the wire and the base of the shell. Cut three small pointed leaves from the rolled-out clay. Attach by pressing ends into the clay around the triton base. Make six triton buds in this fashion. Let air-dry.

12 For flower centers, form and flatten small rounds of clay; incise clay with a pencil point, or add small flattened blobs of

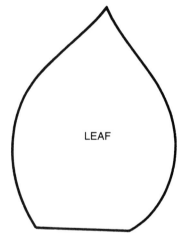

LEAF

clay, or run clay through a garlic press, forming a small cluster as it emerges from the press. Let air-dry.

13 To make the bow and streamers, roll out more clay to the thickness of thin piecrust. Run a paring knife against a ruler's edge to cut out six strips ⅛ inch wide by 7 inches long for loops, and another three strips ⅛ inch wide by 10 inches long for streamers. Follow the photograph to form the loops and streamers, pressing them together where they meet at the center. Use rolls of aluminum foil to support the loops while they are drying. Remove these supports when the loops are almost dry, so the surfaces are exposed to air.

14 If oven-drying clay has been used, once everything has air-dried thoroughly, place the pieces on baking pans and warm them in a 150° oven. Then bake them for an hour in a 250° oven with the door open a crack, or follow the clay manufacturer's directions.

15 After everything has been dried or baked, prime the surfaces with the white latex paint. Let dry thoroughly.

16 Paint the flowers, centers, and leaves with acrylic paint in desired colors. Shading is simple, usually just a second color with softened edges.

17 Paint the baby's breath clusters white.

18 Paint the shell rosebuds rosy red with green leaves and stems.

19 Paint the ribbons pearlized white.

20 Attach the centers to the flowers, using a glue gun. Often the hot glue will not stick where there is paint, so sand the paint away first.

21 Assemble the wreath by gluing the ribbon on first, and then build out from there with flowers and leaves, sanding away any paint that might impede adherence.

22 Apply several light coats of the lacquer spray to give the wreath a glossy sheen.

Designer's Note

Although patterns for two flowers and a leaf are provided, flower shapes can also be cut out of clay freehand with a knife or cookie cutters. The flower details are hand-formed and added afterward, which is what gives this wreath its charm. Designer Ellen Jane Ferrell suggests making the flowers, leaves, and ribbons ahead of time and storing them for later use.

For her own wreaths, she works on a wooden table easel with variously spaced nails to hold the wreath upright at a proper angle for attaching the clay decorations.

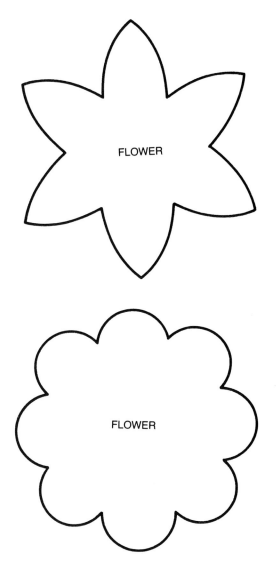

HYDRANGEAS ON SHOW

What makes this wreath so special is the fresh country look it achieves with homegrown flowers. Beautiful as it is, it can be made with little effort in three to five hours and at little cost.

Liz Reilly's first wreath was one she made a few years ago for a church bazaar. Since then she's been making four to five wreaths a year, either as gifts or to sell at Christmas bazaars.

Liz is married, with five children ranging in age from two and a half to twelve years. She works part-time, volunteers at her children's school, and likes to sew and garden.

TO MAKE THE WREATH

1 If the straw wreath is covered with plastic, remove the plastic wrapping.

2 Attach a hanger to the base (see How to Hang Your Wreath, page 149).

3 Attach the hydrangea clusters to the wreath with the glue gun, completely covering the top and sides. If necessary, shorten the stems first.

4 Wire the small baby's breath clusters together for ease in handling. To attach them and the rest of the dried flowers to the wreath, dab hot glue on the stem at the base of each flower or cluster and tuck it into the hydrangeas; if necessary, clip the stems first.

5 Form the sixteen ribbon roses (See How to Make Rolled Ribbon Roses, page 50).

6 Glue the ribbon roses in at random around the wreath.

7 From the blue ribbon, form a bow with twelve loops, each 3¾ inches wide (see To Form a Starburst Bow, page 152). Glue a 2-inch round of ribbon in the center of the loops (see To Form a Ribbon Round, page 151).

8 Glue the bow to the top of the wreath.

9 Spray the wreath with glitter, to highlight the flowers and give the whole work an extra sparkle.

SIZE
Approximately 19" diameter

BASE
16"-diameter straw wreath

MATERIALS AND TOOLS
16 rose-pink ribbon roses, 1" wide (can be purchased or made)
Dried flowers (see How to Dry Flowers and Other Naturals, page 157): blue and green hydrangeas separated into small clusters, white strawflowers, miniature red roses, globe amaranth, xeranthemum, small clusters of baby's breath
4½ yards rose-pink satin ribbon, ⅞" wide, to make ribbon roses
3 yards bright-blue satin ribbon, ⅞" wide
Floral wire
Wire cutters
Garden shears
Scissors
Glue gun
Daisy Kingdom Holiday Glitter Spray

Liz Reilly of Portland, Oregon

HOW TO MAKE ROLLED RIBBON ROSES

1 Cut the rose-pink ribbon into sixteen 10-inch lengths. Cut sixteen 4-inch lengths of floral wire.

2 To make each ribbon rose, lay a ribbon length with the satin side down (the light side in the diagrams). Fold the right tail over the left, forming a right angle and leaving a 1-inch tail (see Figure 1).

3 For the center bud, tightly roll the ribbon two turns to your left, or until the shiny tail is rolled up (see Figure 2).

4 Fold the top of the ribbon back and under (see Figure 3).

5 While holding the tail firmly, roll the bud a half-turn to the left (see Figure 4); the bud is starting to turn into a flower.

6 Again fold the top of the ribbon back and under, and roll the flower a half-turn to the left (see Figure 5).

7 Continue to fold the top of the ribbon back and under and to roll the flower a half-turn to the left as in Figure 5, until there is only about 1 inch of ribbon tail left (see Figure 6); the rose will be fully formed.

8 Hold the tail and stem together and wrap them with the previously cut floral wire; twist the wire to hold. Then wind green floral tape around the stem.

Designer's Note

According to Liz Reilly, hydrangeas are easy to dry. Pick them in the late summer or early fall, and hang them upside down or put them in a vase without water. They will dry in ten days to two weeks.

Keep them in a warm, dry room because they absorb moisture easily and lose their color.

After the hydrangeas are dried, carefully separate the flowers into small clusters for use in the wreath.

Liz Reilly uses no preservative spray because she believes sprays for preserving dried flowers can get sticky and attract dust.

She makes her own ribbon roses because she has found it difficult to get a good color match between dried flowers and available ribbons.

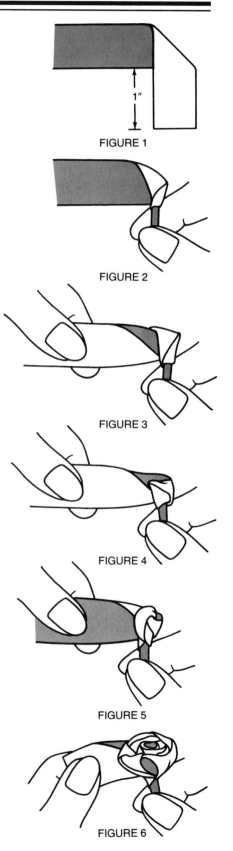

FIGURE 1

FIGURE 2

FIGURE 3

FIGURE 4

FIGURE 5

FIGURE 6

TULIPS FOR ALL SEASONS

The superb arrangement of flowers fashioned from corn husks claimed Second Prize for this wreath.

Margaret Butcher of Ojai, California

Peggy Butcher is a full-time homemaker now, having previously operated a cottage business selling corn-husk crafts.

She has always enjoyed creating in one medium or another. She started teaching at age sixteen as the art director of her local Girls' Club of America and more recently gave arts and crafts classes at a local gift shop.

She has been married for eleven years and has two daughters at home: Nina, ten, and Emily, two.

This particular wreath was made for Tender Life, her favorite nonprofit organization, for their annual fund-raising silent auction.

TO MAKE THE WREATH

1 For the base, form two 13-inch rings from coat hangers or clothesline wire. Let the ends overlap and wrap them with floral wire to hold. Wire rings together.

2 Attach a hanger to the base (see How to Hang Your Wreath, page 149).

3 Make a pattern for the tulip petal by cutting a curve along one narrow end of the cardboard.

4 Soak the corn husks in water for about a half-hour, then carefully take them apart. (**Note:** It is very important that corn husks be kept damp and pliable while you are working with them.)

5 Dye about fifteen husks rose pink, following dye package directions.

6 Use your petal pattern to cut out seventy-two petals from the dampened husks.

7 With the wide end of the egg down, evenly space six petals around it, allowing about 1¼ inches at the bottom to gather in, and wrap with wire. Let the petals dry before removing the egg. Continue until you have twelve tulips.

8 Dye about eleven husks denim blue. While they are still damp, use the petal pattern to cut out fifty-four petals.

9 Follow Step 7 to make nine tulips.

10 For stems, dye from twelve to fifteen husks Kelly green. While still damp, cut or tear the entire length of the green-dyed husk into 2-inch widths.

SIZE
Approximately 17" diameter

BASE
13"-diameter wire ring

MATERIALS AND TOOLS
Approximately 80 corn
    husks
Rit Liquid Fabric Dye: rose
    pink, denim blue, Kelly
    green
12 plastic-foam eggs
Thin cardboard, 2¼" × 4"
Galvanized clothesline wire,
    or 2 wire coat hangers
    with hooks cut off
Floral wire
Wire cutters
Scissors
Curling iron
Clear acrylic gloss spray
    sealer

11 To attach stems to each tulip, place a pair of green husks over each tulip stem, facing up and covering the tulip. Wrap wire around each stem. Flip the husk stems down and wrap them with wire again.

12 Continue until all the tulips have stems.

13 For leaves, dye from twenty-eight to thirty husks Kelly green. While still damp, cut or tear the entire length of the husks into seventy-five to eighty 3-inch widths. Cut a point at one end of the leaf. (**Note:** Cutting can be facilitated by stacking the husks and doing several at a time.)

14 While the leaves are still damp, attach them in a clockwise direction to the wire ring base, using floral wire. Use a heated curling iron to make the damp corn husks look like tulip leaves.

15 Tuck the dried tulips between the leaves and wire them in place.

16 After the wreath has dried, spray it with the sealer to give it luster.

AUTUMN HARVEST

Here is turn-of-the-century opulence, an exuberant expression of autumn that could add distinction to any front door or enhance any room.

Pam Hoover of Modesto, California

Pam Hoover works out of her home as a silk-floral designer. Her arrangements, wreaths, sprays, plants, and trees sell to stores and interior decorators. Much of her work is customized, coordinating with fabrics and wallpapers.

"As a single mother of an eight-year-old daughter and a three-year-old son, I am able to be both a homemaker and businesswoman."

With an art-major background, she takes special satisfaction in working with both silk and dried flowers. Her training also shows in the sure sense with which she has arranged her materials to create a wreath with great dimension.

TO MAKE THE WREATH

1 Attach a hanger to the base (see How to Hang Your Wreath, page 149).

2 Form a bow from the untwisted paper twist with four 6-inch loops and two streamers, 18 inches long on the right and 24 inches on the left. (See To Form a French Bow, page 154. However, begin with a 6-inch round.)

3 Glue the bow to the upper left of the wreath. Trail the streamers to the right and left of the bow, swirling and gluing them where they touch the grapevine.

4 Starting and ending behind the bow, swirl the ivy leaf runner around the wreath and glue to hold here and there.

5 Arrange the five bunches of grapes, two on each side of the bow and one hanging from the bottom of the wreath. Glue in place.

6 Glue the two sprigs of miniature morning glories so they sprout outward from each side of the bow.

7 Glue the berry stems and cut-up clusters of hydrangeas at random around the wreath.

8 Softly mist the wreath with gold spray.

9 Form a bow from the wire-edge metallic ribbon with two 4½-inch loops and two 12-inch streamers (see To Form a Two-Loop Bow, page 152).

10 Glue the metallic bow next to the paper-twist bow. Swirl and twist the streamers.

SIZE
Approximately 22" diameter

BASE
20"-diameter bleached grapevine wreath

MATERIALS AND TOOLS
Artificial silk flowers, berries, leaves, and grapes: 7 bunches shiny and matte grapes; 5 bunches large and small berries; 2 yards ivy leaf runners with 2"– 4" leaves; 2 sprigs periwinkle-blue miniature morning glories; hydrangeas separated into 6 clusters
5 stems live pepper berries
2¾ yards mauve paper twist
1½ yards wire-edge gold metallic ribbon, 1½" wide
Scissors
Glue gun
Gold metallic spray

A ROUND OF OAK LEAVES

Here is an easy way to create truly everlasting autumn foliage!

Jacqueline Misek of Westmont, Illinois

Jacqueline Misek, who before this had made only two other wreaths, also enjoys needlepoint and beadwork.

In addition to these hobbies, she is treasurer of the Westmont town festival and the Veterans of Foreign Wars Auxiliary and is an active member of the First Christian Church of Downers Grove.

Jacqueline finds time in her busy schedule to collect butterflies, and her wreath was inspired by her desire to create a fall decoration for her door—hence the oak-leaf motif.

TO MAKE THE WREATH

1 Attach a hanger to the base (see How to Hang Your Wreath, page 149).

2 Spray all fabrics with Scotch-gard; let dry.

3 For the leaves, pair fabrics of different patterns, joining each pair with the fusible web, following package directions. Use the tracing paper to trace the triple oak leaf (see pattern).

4 With transfer paper, trace the outlines onto cardboard, making several patterns. (The designer cut six, enabling her to lay out the most leaves from her fabric lengths without wasting material.) Lay patterns very closely together on the fused fabrics. Use the pencil or marker to trace around them. Keep moving the patterns and tracing around them until forty sets of triple leaves are drawn. Carefully cut out the leaves.

5 With the letter opener, make a slit in the plastic wreath; squirt several drops of glue into the slit. Then, again using the letter opener, push the stem center of the leaves into the slit. Continue to make slits approximately 6 inches apart, filling them until the sides and top of the wreath are completely and evenly covered with leaves.

6 Finish trimming the wreath by making small slits in the foam, adding glue, and then inserting the stems of the miniature acorns and pumpkins into the slots.

SIZE
Approximately 13" diameter

BASE
12"-diameter green plastic-foam wreath

MATERIALS AND TOOLS
10 quarter-yard pieces of cotton fabric, cut from 45" widths, in solids, plaids, calicos, and small prints in autumn colors
5 bunches artificial acorns
9 miniature pumpkins
1 yard fusible web
3 shirt cardboards
Tracing paper
Transfer paper
Pencil
Tacky glue
Letter opener
Scissors
Iron
Scotch-gard Fabric Protector

OAK LEAF CLUSTER

Designer's Note

Although Jacqueline Misek used a spray to protect the fabric, her wreath is not weatherproof, so she hangs it on the inside of her door. She also notes that you could use holly leaves in shades of green for a Christmas wreath, or flowers in pastel colors for spring.

VEGETABLE FANTASY

Paper twist produces this spectacular bouquet of vegetables, a tour de force showing great ingenuity and craftsmanship on the designer's part. She has, in fact, been perfecting her technique with paper twist for a year or so, and with crafts in general for nine years.

Kathy Zawacki of Toledo, Ohio

Kathy Zawacki's winning wreath is based on one that was six feet in diameter. A caterer had spotted her paper vegetables at a crafts show and asked her to do a Thanksgiving banquet display. First she twisted a grapevine wreath to fit the six-foot space she had to fill. (No small feat in itself!) Then she filled the wreath with paper-twist-covered cabbages, tomatoes, pumpkins, carrots, onions, and cauliflower, with a large raffia bow for accent. The results brought her still more business!

Kathy Zawacki's is a unique success story: She gave up a part-time job to devote her entire time to Simple Pleasures, as she calls her business, and she now sells her work through wholesale channels, gift markets, and home parties. A staff of three friends helps her assemble her designs. Also lending a hand are her husband, Gary, and her children (Amy, twenty, and Jeremy, sixteen).

TO MAKE THE WREATH

1 Attach a hanger to the base (see How to Hang Your Wreath, page 149).

2 Make four tomatoes, using the 4-inch plastic-foam balls. Cut the red paper twist into 14-inch lengths. Untwist the paper and use two or more lengths to enclose the foam ball, bringing the paper to meet at the top. Glue the paper twist flat where the ends meet. Cut away any excess paper. Continue until each ball is entirely covered.

3 To make the stems, cut the hunter green paper twist into four lengths, each 1½ inches long. Fan out one end of each twist, flatten it, and cut it into a round. Use this flattened end to glue a stem to each tomato.

4 Make three large onions, using the 3½-inch plastic-foam balls. Cut the white paper twist into 14-inch lengths. Untwist the paper and use two or more lengths to enclose each foam ball. Allow the excess to come together and form the top of the onion. Glue and twist the onion ends together; clip them into wide notches. Glue a small clump of excelsior to the bottom of each onion to finish it.

5 Make five medium onions, using the 3-inch-high plastic-foam eggs. Cut the white paper twist into 10-inch lengths. Untwist the paper and use two or more lengths to enclose each foam egg. Complete the tops and bottoms in the same way as the large onions (Step 4).

6 To make six carrots, cut six lengths of orange paper twist, each 18 inches long. Untwist the paper and fold each piece in half lengthwise. With the fold at the bottom, wrap the paper twist around crushed tissue paper to form a carrot that is wider at the

SIZE
Approximately 26" diameter

BASE
24"-diameter grapevine wreath

MATERIALS AND TOOLS
Paper twist: red, deep red, hunter green, gray green, orange, white
3 plastic-foam balls, 4½" diameter; 4 balls, 4" diameter; 3 balls, 3½" diameter
5 plastic-foam eggs, 3" high
3 clusters white yarrow, 3½" wide
Excelsior
2 yards raffia
Tissue-paper scraps
Pencil
Scissors
Curling iron (optional)
Glue gun

top and twisted tightly at the bottom. Leave 1 inch of the paper twist unstuffed at the top end. Twist it tightly and glue to hold.

7 For the carrot greens, cut twelve 12-inch lengths from the hunter green paper twist. Untwist them and cut a point at one end of each piece; then cut a series of alternating slanting snips on the long edges, stopping 1½ inches from the straight end. Wrap, twist, and glue two "leaves" to each carrot end. Let the "greens" dangle.

8 To make four chili peppers, cut four 6-inch lengths of deep red paper twist. Untwist them and wrap each piece around tissue paper, forming a pepper that is wider at the top and twisted tightly at the bottom. Leave 1 inch of the paper twist unstuffed at the top end. Twist it tightly and glue to hold.

9 To make the pepper stems, cut the hunter green paper twist into four 3-inch lengths. Fan out one end of each twist; fit and glue it over the pepper end.

10 Make three cabbages, using the 4½-inch plastic-foam balls. Cut the gray-green paper twist into enough 15½-inch lengths to cover the balls. Untwist and use two or more pieces to enclose each foam ball, bringing the paper up to meet at the top; glue the paper twist flat where the ends meet. Cut away any excess paper. Continue until each ball is entirely covered.

11 For ten leaves for each cabbage, cut thirty 6-inch lengths of gray-green paper twist. Untwist them and cut a curve along one narrow end of each piece. Arrange a pair of leaves on either side of each cabbage, with the narrow straight ends at the bottom. Gather slightly to fit and glue to hold at the bottom. Glue two more leaves in between the first two and then glue on another two. Arrange and glue four more leaves. Curl back the curved edges of the outer leaves over a pencil (or use a curling iron).

12 Make three cauliflowers, using a 3½-inch cluster of dried yarrow as a center for each. For leaves for each cauliflower, cut eight 6-inch lengths of paper twist: four of hunter green and four of gray-green. Untwist paper and cut a curve along one narrow end. Follow the photograph to arrange the leaves around the yarrow, and tie them together under the flower cluster with a piece of raffia. Curl some of the leaf edges over a pencil. (Or use a curling iron.)

13 Arrange the vegetables around the wreath and glue them in place one by one.

14 From the raffia form a bow with two 6-inch loops and two 20-inch streamers (see To Form a Two-Loop Bow, page 152). Glue this on top of the vegetables on the upper right of the wreath. Let the streamers trail around the wreath and glue here and there to hold.

ROSES AND RIBBONS

Delicate as this wreath looks, it is durable, for the roses are fashioned from bread dough. They are bug-resistant and, unless it is exposed to extreme moisture, the wreath will last for years.

Norma J. Rudloff of Lagrangeville, New York

Norma Rudloff has established herself as a professional craftsperson. Up until 1982 she worked with her husband. That year he decided to give up the business. It was also the year that her youngest daughter (Norma has three children and two grandchildren) was going off to college. She answered the question "What do I do now?" by making dolls and selling them at crafts shows. But she also started dabbling with salt-dough ornaments, and when they outsold the dolls, she branched out with wreaths and other floral arrangements featuring her roses. She is a member of the Hudson Valley Artisans' Guild and shows regularly at crafts fairs in the Northeast.

TO MAKE THE WREATH

1 If the straw wreath is covered with plastic, remove the plastic wrapping.

2 Attach a hanger to the base (see How to Hang Your Wreath, page 149).

3 From the bread dough recipe on page 64, make the roses and the rosebuds: Start by forming a curled center bud and then build up petals around it. The size of the rose depends on the number of petals; a bud can have three and a large rose thirteen. Add or subtract petals to get the size rose needed.

4 Spread a piece of aluminum foil on the work surface. If possible, look at a real rose while working with the dough.

5 From the bag of pink dough, take a small amount to work with. From this take a very small piece and roll it between the palms of both hands to form a ball the size of a small pea (about ¼ inch diameter).

6 Press the dough "pea" into a flat round. To achieve a delicate porcelain look, it is important the dough round be pressed as thin as paper.

7 Form a center bud by rolling up this round from right to left, making the bottom of the round slightly tighter than the top so the bud looks as if it is about to open.

8 For the first petal follow Steps 5 and 6.

9 Roll back the top left and top right sides of the petal (as though the petal is curling).

10 Lay the bud in the middle of the petal so the petal is slightly higher and wrap the petal around the base of the bud.

SIZE
Approximately 15″ diameter

BASE
14″-diameter straw wreath

MATERIALS AND TOOLS
Pink bread-dough roses
(see Bread Dough recipe
p. 64): 5 large, 1¼″
wide; 10 medium,
1″ wide; 5 mini roses, ¾″
wide
Eucalyptus in small clusters
75 clusters of baby's breath
15 artificial silk rose leaves
1½ yards medium-rose
satin ribbon, ⅛″ wide
Spool of 28-gauge green
floral wire
Wire cutters
Tacky glue
Aluminum foil
Glue gun

11 Repeat Steps 5, 6, and 9 for the second petal; place it opposite the first petal and wrap it around the bud and first petal.

12 Follow Steps 5, 6, and 9 to add three more petals; overlap them around the bud and original petals.

13 Continue to make more petals to achieve the size rose needed by following Steps 5, 6, and 9.

14 Let the rose air-dry on the foil for at least twelve hours.

15 Make as many roses as you need; let them air-dry.

16 Completely cover the top and sides of the wreath with eucalyptus clumps, attaching them with a glue gun.

17 Glue the baby's breath clusters here and there around the wreath.

18 Position the dough roses and glue them to the wreath with tacky glue.

19 Place the silk rose leaves near the roses and attach them with a glue gun.

20 Follow the photograph to wind the ribbon around the wreath.

BREAD DOUGH RECIPE
(makes about 24 large roses)

1 Crumble bread into small pieces, place in a mixing bowl, and add the rest of the ingredients, except the paint.

2 Knead the mixture until the ingredients come together and are smooth. It is important that the bread be worked into the dough and that the dough is completely smooth and pliable like Play-Doh.

3 During the first several minutes, the dough will be very sticky, but after more kneading it can be handled without sticking. **Note:** If the dough is too moist, add a bit more cornstarch; if too dry, add a few more drops of lemon juice. Knead the added ingredients into the dough.

4 To color the dough, pour a small amount of liquid acrylic paint into the center of the dough, and continue kneading until the color is blended in. Add paint as necessary until the right intensity of color is achieved.

5 If more than one color is being used, keep each colored ball of dough in a separate, sealed plastic bag.

6 If not using the dough right away, store the plastic bags in a refrigerator or freezer to prevent the dough from drying out.

INGREDIENTS
16 slices white bread with crusts removed
Aleene's Tacky Glue, 8-ounce bottle
¼ cup lemon juice
1 cup cornstarch
1 tablespoon Pond's Cold Cream
Liquid acrylic paint, rose pink

WITH A THOUGHT
FOR CHILDREN

BOO! IT'S HALLOWEEN

Why shouldn't a wreath just be fun, like this whimsical celebration of Halloween? It's one the kids can help to assemble, and when the witches' night is over, the base can be retrimmed . . . for Thanksgiving, then for Christmas.

Susan Sanville of Worthington, Ohio

Susan Sanville makes wreaths for her front door every month, but the Halloween wreath is the family favorite, what with three boys at home aged two, five, and twelve. At the end of September, Susan takes down her autumn wreath (an 18-inch grapevine decorated with dried flowers, leaves, and pinecones), stores the materials in a labeled bag, and retrieves the makings of Halloween from another bag.

She uses three basic grapevine wreaths for the entire year—the 22-inch one shown here, an oval, and a bleached grapevine base—and she usually wires the decorative items to the base, rather than gluing them, so the wreath can be readily disassembled.

Her special pleasure in wreath-making derives from her finding that "it offers free-form fun—there are no mistakes to correct. If something doesn't look as I've planned, I can easily change it."

TO MAKE THE WREATH

1 Make a drying form for the ghosts, by pinning a wax-paper ball to the top of each plastic-foam cone (one for each ghost). Place these forms on a layer of newspapers or a piece of wax paper to protect the work surface.

2 With pinking shears, cut the white fabric into three 8-inch squares.

3 Pour the draping medium into the pie plate and submerge the fabric, saturating it thoroughly.

4 Wring out the fabric and drape each piece over a prepared form. Let it dry for twenty-four to forty-eight hours.

5 When the ghosts are dry, pull them off the forms and remove the wax-paper balls. Hot-glue a craft stick inside each ghost.

6 For pumpkins, use the serrated knife to cut one ball in half. Then, to make these two halves and the whole ball look like pumpkins, contour them by cutting deep grooves in them with the knife point.

7 Brush the pumpkins with white glue, coating them well. Cover each one in a round of orange paper twist cut big enough to enclose it. Draw the edges up to the top of the pumpkins, following its contours. Cut away any excess.

8 Cut three 1-inch lengths of brown paper twist for stems. From flat green paper twist, cut three small square pieces for leaves and roll three narrow, tightly twisted brown pieces around a pencil, one at a time, for vines.

9 Push one leaf, a stem, and a vine into the top of each pumpkin, and glue.

10 Attach a hanger to the base (see How to Hang Your Wreath, page 149).

SIZE
Approximately 22" diameter

BASE
22"-diameter grapevine wreath

MATERIALS AND TOOLS
White cotton fabric, 9" × 27"
3¼ yards orange open-weave ribbon, 3" wide
Paper twist: 1 yard each orange and black; ½ yard each green and brown
Shredded corn husks
Excelsior
Orange paper raffia
2 plastic-foam balls, 4" diameter
3 plastic-foam cones
White glue
Flat brush
Bottle of liquid draping medium
Wax paper
Aluminum-foil pie plate
Craft sticks
Floral wire
Scissors
Pinking shears
Wire cutters
Serrated kitchen knife
Straight pins
Glue gun

11 Following the photograph, arrange the excelsior mixed with the orange raffia along the bottom of the wreath; attach them with a glue gun.

12 Position the ghosts by inserting their craft sticks into the excelsior and hot-gluing them in place.

13 Arrange the pumpkins around the ghosts (the whole pumpkin is in front, slightly tipped forward) and hot-glue.

14 Form a 7-inch "haystack" from shredded corn husks; hot-glue behind a ghost.

15 Open the black paper twist and softly drape it across the top left of the wreath; attach with a glue gun.

16 From the orange open-weave ribbon, form a bow with eight 4½-inch loops, with a 12-inch streamer on the left and a 22-inch streamer on the right (see To Form a French Bow, page 154).

17 Arrange the bow on the upper left of the wreath over the black swag, looping the streamers and hot-gluing them in place.

JOLLY SNOWMEN AND FRIENDS

Here's a designer who brainstorms when she shops and makes a merry, pretty mixup of whatever catches her eye.

Susie Light of Winfield, Kansas

Susie Light and her husband, Steve, love to boat and fish and go sightseeing in their Cessna. They have been married for twenty years and "raise English setters instead of children." She also works part-time for a local pharmacy.

But Susie's dream is someday to work out of her home "on a regular basis, selling my wreath and floral designs under the name Silksations."

TO MAKE THE WREATH

1 For the base, look for an evenly shaped grapevine wreath with many curly tendrils. The hidden ones on the back of the wreath can be cut off to be glued here and there on the front after the wreath is finished.

2 Attach a hanger to the base (see How to Hang Your Wreath, page 149).

3 From the wider flocked ribbon form a bow with twelve 4-inch loops (see To Form a Starburst Bow, page 152). Repeat with the plaid ribbon. Also cut from each of these ribbons a pair of 18-inch streamers, which will be glued to the wreath later.

4 Glue the plaid bow on top of the flocked bow.

5 Glue this double bow to the upper left of the wreath. (When making a pair of wreaths for double doors, place the ribbons on the right for a right-hand door and to the left for the left door.)

6 To make the flat metal ornaments stand out and appear to float, glue one or two thicknesses of small cardboard pieces to their backs.

7 Position the ornaments on the wreath and then pick them up one by one and hot-glue them in place.

8 Glue a pine piece topped with a red bell on each ornament.

9 Cut the narrow flocked ribbon into 18-inch lengths.

10 Starting under the bow, and using tweezers or pliers, pull a ribbon length through the grapevine, weaving and looping it, gluing where necessary, and ending under an ornament.

11 Start a new ribbon length under an ornament and continue around the wreath until the ribbon is used up, ending under the bow.

12 Glue on the holly leaves, hiding their ends under the ornaments or ribbons; have some appear to be sprouting from between the grapevines.

SIZE
Approximately 20" diameter

BASE
18"-diameter grapevine wreath

MATERIALS AND TOOLS
White enameled flat metal ornaments 4" high: 2 snowmen, 2 bears, 2 reindeer
Red flocked ribbons: 3¾ yards each, 1¼" wide and ¾" wide
3¾ yards plaid taffeta ribbon, 1½" wide
8 small pinecones, ¼" diameter
17 white berry clumps, each holding 5 berries, ⅜" diameter
11 red berries, ⅜" diameter
50 artificial silk holly leaves
6 pieces artificial pine
6 red bells, ⅜" diameter
Cardboard
White liquid acrylic paint
Flat sponge brush, 1" wide
Flat dish
White paper towels
Floral wire
Wire cutters
Tweezers or needlenose pliers
Scissors
Glue gun

13 Glue on the berries and berry clusters; bend them around the wreath and ornaments.

14 Give the pinecones a touch of "snow": Dip the foam brush lightly into the white acrylic paint, remove the excess on a paper towel, and dab the tips of the pinecone scales.

15 After the paint dries, glue a red berry to the tip of each pinecone and then hot-glue the pinecone to the wreath.

16 Follow the photographs to arrange the previously cut plaid and velour streamers under each side of the bow. Attach the streamers to the outer edges of the wreath by rippling the ribbons and gluing them every 2½ to 3 inches, leaving the last 3 inches loose and unglued. Cut inverted notches at the ends.

Designer's Note

As one who has made many wreaths, Susie Light advises, "Build a wreath to last. Be sure ornaments and berries will stay in place if displayed on a high-traffic door by wiggling them slightly after the hot glue has cooled; reglue where loose."

BALLOONS FOR BIRTHDAYS

This decoration could become a family tradition, along with the birthday cake and ice cream that we all love.

Kay Dugger of Georgetown, Illinois

Kay Dugger was inspired to create this wreath when she saw a little girl with a balloon barrette. She is a crafter who learns either by looking at pictures or just trying and retrying "till I get it right." She works part-time as a librarian. Kay has a husband and three children, two boys in high school and a daughter in the sixth grade.

TO MAKE THE WREATH

1 If the straw base is covered with plastic, remove the plastic wrapping.

2 Attach a hanger to the base (see How To Hang Your Wreath, page 149).

3 Use the floral U-pins to attach the balloons through their middle to the top and sides of the wreath so it is completely covered.

4 Cut three 24-inch lengths from each color curling ribbon.

5 Tie ribbons around the horn and curl ends on a scissors blade.

6 Use wire to attach the horn to the wreath; do the same with the Happy Birthday sign and the plastic mini-balloon party favor.

7 Cut the rest of the ribbon into 8-inch lengths. Curl ribbons on the scissors blade and attach them with the floral U-pins throughout the wreath.

SIZE
Approximately 13" diameter

BASE
11"-diameter straw wreath

MATERIALS AND TOOLS
250–300 balloons in assorted colors
Party favors, including pink plastic Happy Birthday sign, 3" wide; cluster of plastic balloons, each balloon 1" diameter; and party horn
Curling ribbon ¼" wide, 3 yards each yellow, red, Wedgwood blue
Scissors
250–300 floral U-pins
Floral wire
Wire cutters

HOORAY FOR THE RED, WHITE, AND BLUE

"I hang this wreath on my classroom door during February," says this winner, a first-grade teacher. "But I also made one for a lady who put it on her grandpa's grave on Memorial Day."

TO MAKE THE WREATH

1 With a compass, draw a 4½-inch circle on the cardboard; cut out.

2 Arrange the flags on the back of the circle, all facing the same direction, with their pole ends touching; hot-glue in place.

3 Cut eleven 7½-inch lengths from the white ribbon, six 7½-inch lengths from red, six 7½-inch lengths and three 13-inch lengths from the navy.

4 Turn the cardboard over and cover the circle with the 7½-inch ribbons, crisscrossing them and attaching them with the glue gun.

5 With the three longer navy ribbons, form two-loop bows (see instructions on page 152) and glue them on top of the crisscrossed ribbon as shown in the photograph.

6 Attach a hanger to the base (see How to Hang Your Wreath, page 149).

SIZE
Approximately 22" diameter

BASE
4½"-diameter circle of cardboard

MATERIALS AND TOOLS
12 American flags, 4" × 6½" with 10" poles
Satin ribbon, ⅜" wide: 1½ yards red, 2½ yards white, 2½ yards navy
Thin cardboard, 5" square
Compass
Scissors
Glue gun

Dawn Geppert of Sturgis, South Dakota

Dawn Geppert has made almost 100 different wreaths, each one unique. She exhibits at bazaars and fairs and teaches crafts classes for all age groups. "My husband always knows where I am," she says. "If I'm not at school, or at home working on crafts, I'm at a crafts store or crafts show."

HANDS AND HEARTS

Nine grandchildren visit the Dawsons on holidays, and "I try to make the house decor fit their dreams as to what a holiday at Grandma's and Grandpa's is." Sometimes the theme celebrates Valentine's Day, sometimes Mother's Day, sometimes Christmas.

Christabelle Dawson of Rushville, Indiana

A childhood memory inspired this wreath of Christabelle Dawson's. At the church her family attended, they often sang a familiar old hymn by Ada R. Habershon, "Will the Circle Be Unbroken?" For young Christabelle this evoked a picture of her family as a circle of people, bound by Christian love not only on earth but in an unbroken circle for all eternity.

Christabelle Dawson has made wreaths for many years, first as a World War II bride when she whipped Ivory Snow flakes to decorate her outdoor Christmas wreath. She then worked as a clerk-typist in the Selective Service office and the office of Price Administration, while her husband served with General Patton's infantry in Europe.

She operated a tractor, helping to plant and harvest soybeans and corn on the Dawsons' seventy-four-acre farm until they leased it. She is still an outdoors person, and she and her husband drive a motor home and travel a good deal. She's the bookkeeper for their Dawson Soft Water business, and she's deep into a five-year Bible study course.

TO MAKE THE WREATH

1 Bake cookies, at least nine right hands and eight left hands, plus ten hearts, using the cookie recipe on page 78. (**Note:** You might bake more than you need, in case of breakage.)

2 When the cookies have cooled, paint family member names on each hand; let dry.

3 With the compass, draw a 16-inch-diameter circle on the cardboard. Draw another circle in the center, measuring 14½ inches in diameter.

4 Cut the ring from the cardboard with the utility knife or scissors.

5 To cover the cardboard ring, lay the 55-inch felt strip flat on the work surface, with the ring on top of it. To enclose the ring with the felt, fold the borders of the felt up over the ring, easing and pinning as you go, overlapping the long edges on the back. Secure the overlap with small running stitches, to hold the felt firmly in place.

6 Attach a hanger to the base (see How to Hang Your Wreath, page 149).

7 Arrange the cookie hands around the wreath; attach them one by one with the glue gun.

8 Glue on the holly and berries as shown in the photograph.

SIZE
Approximately 18″ diameter

BASE
16″-diameter cardboard ring covered in felt

MATERIALS AND TOOLS
Corrugated cardboard or foamcore, 17″ square
Red felt strips: One 4″ × 55″, one ⅝″ × 24″
Cookies (see cookie recipe, page 78): 9 right hands, 8 left hands, 10 small heart shapes
Artificial holly: 9 single leaves, 9 double leaves with berries
Merry Christmas sign, approximately 5″ × 11″
Needle and red thread
Straight pins
Liquid acrylic paints, Christmas red and green
Artist's brush
Compass
Scissors
Utility knife
Glue gun

9 Cut the 24-inch felt strip in half. Glue the resulting 12-inch strips to the top back of the wreath.

10 Glue two heart cookies to the top of each strip, then glue the Merry Christmas sign; finish by gluing on the remaining six cookies.

HANDS AND HEARTS COOKIE RECIPE

1 Beat margarine and sugar in a large bowl with electric mixer until light in color. Beat in egg and vanilla.

2 Gradually beat in flour and salt until blended. Divide dough in half. Wrap each half in plastic wrap and refrigerate one hour, or until firm enough to roll out.

3 Heat oven to 375°. Have ungreased cookie sheets ready.

4 On lightly floured surface with floured rolling pin, roll half the dough at a time to ¼-inch thickness.

5 Cut dough with hand- and heart-shaped cookie cutters. Also cut out and remove the hearts on the hands at this stage. To be sure you have enough hearts that hold their shape, cut ten more small hearts from a separate sheet of dough. Place all cookies 1 inch apart on cookie sheets.

6 Bake 11 to 13 minutes, or until lightly browned at edges. Remove to wire racks to cool completely.

INGREDIENTS AND UTENSILS
Cookie cutters: hand-
  shape, about 3½" high;
  heart-shape,
  approximately 1" high
1½ cups margarine, at
  room temperature
1 cup granulated sugar
1 large egg
1 teaspoon vanilla extract
4 cups all-purpose flour
½ teaspoon salt

THE TWINKLING SANTAS

David, six, and Maggie, three-and-a-half, helped with this First Prize wreath. David's final check made sure each Santa has a twinkle in his eyes.

Indy Bacon of Hartland, Michigan

Indy Bacon credits her craftsmanship to heredity, only secondarily to her art major at college. Her mother, sisters, aunts, uncle, grandfather, and grandmother were all artists or crafters. She herself works in stained glass, fabric painting, stenciling, rag baskets, and needle arts as well as wreath-making. She is an active volunteer with the Junior League of Flint, Michigan, and loves cross-country skiing and camping. But her saying is, "Busy hands, happy heart: Only dull women have immaculate houses, and she who dies with the most crafts supplies wins!"

DRIFTWOOD SANTAS
APPROXIMATE SIZE

TO MAKE THE WREATH

1 For the base: Draw an 11-inch circle with the compass on the wood paneling or Masonite. In the center draw an 8-inch circle.

2 Cut out the ring with the jigsaw (see Materials and Tools, page 148). If necessary, smooth all edges with sandpaper.

3 Sort the driftwood pieces.

4 Look for the obvious faces and beards, and apply the paint. Use flesh for the faces, white for the beards and mustaches (slightly thinned so the grain comes through), crimson for the hats and bodies, and brown for the areas on the driftwood that are not part of the Santa shape.

5 Draw in the facial features with black paint, using the fine brush (see patterns for examples). Paint the eyes blue; add a white dot to the pupil to make it gleam; use pink for the cheeks.

6 Arrange the Santas around the base, starting with the longer ones and filling in with the shorter, trying for a good balance of shape, size, and color. Use small pieces of the driftwood fillers painted brown under the Santas to build up the wreath where needed.

7 Attach the pieces one by one with the glue gun. For additional strength and adherence, squirt wood glue into as many places as possible under the Santas and the fillers. Let dry.

8 To hang, space the seven screw eyes evenly around the back of the wreath. Run the picture wire through the screw eyes; pull taut and twist wire ends together.

Designer's Note

The entire Bacon family helped gather the driftwood pieces along their beach. The personalities of the Santas were largely determined by the shapes of the wood. The natural weathering created obvious beards, leaving just the faces to be painted.

In order for everyone's favorite Santa to be at the top, seven screw eyes were evenly spaced on the back of the wreath, enabling it to be turned and hung in different positions.

SIZE
Approximately 18" diameter

BASE
11"-diameter wood ring

MATERIALS AND TOOLS
Wood paneling or
    Masonite, 14" square
Driftwood, 1"–7½" long, plus
    small filler pieces
    (approximately 61 pieces
    all together)
Liquid acrylic paints:
    crimson red, flesh, white,
    pink, royal blue, black,
    dark brown
Artist's brushes, medium and
    fine (#00)
Medium sandpaper
Compass
Drill
Jigsaw
7 screw eyes
Picture wire
Wire cutters
Glue gun and woodworking
    glue sticks
Wood glue

A WHEEL OF CRAYONS

This wreath is perfect to brighten a child's room or as a gift for a teacher or librarian. It's a good way to use leftover crayons.

TO MAKE THE WREATH

1 Place the 10-inch hoop on the cardboard and then center the 8-inch hoop in the middle. Tape the hoops to the cardboard in a few places. (The cardboard acts as a turntable, allowing the fixed hoops to be turned as the crayons are being glued. As the work progresses the tape will be removed and the cardboard discarded.)

2 Tape a 6-inch-diameter coffee can or pot in the center of the smaller hoop, to act as a guide to position the crayons evenly all the way around.

3 Place the crayons on the hoops with the points out and all the labels facing up. Arrange them so there is a pleasing sequence of light and dark colors.

4 Hot-glue the crayons to the pair of hoops one by one, as shown in the photograph; at the same time, remove the tape used to attach the hoops to the cardboard.

5 Gently turn the wreath over with the crayons facing down. Add more hot glue to attach the crayons to the hoops from the back.

6 Attach a hanger to the base (see How to Hang Your Wreath, page 149).

7 Cut 5½ inches from each end of the measuring tape for streamers.

8 From the remaining tape, form a bow with fourteen loops, each measuring about 1¾ inches (see To Form a Florist's Bow, page 154).

9 Wire the bow to the wreath.

10 Hot-glue the two 5½-inch streamers under the bow and to the crayons, as shown in the photograph.

SIZE
Approximately 13" diameter

BASE
Two round wood hoops, 8" and 10" in diameter

MATERIALS AND TOOLS
54 crayons in assorted colors
60-inch yellow paper measuring tape
Stiff cardboard, 15" square
Masking tape
Floral wire
Wire cutters
Scissors
Glue gun

Nancy Hayes of Anchorage, Alaska

Nancy Hayes likes to try new crafts and has been doing so for fifteen years. She appliqués and makes wreaths, dolls, and all sorts of decorations, mostly to give as gifts. But as people asked her to make gifts for them to give, she started selling at local bazaars. Now she's back to gifts, because a new part-time job rules out the bazaars.

Her nine-year-old daughter has a crafts basket of her own in Nancy's workroom, where Nancy develops crafts projects for her daughter's class. She helps in her daughter's classroom in school, serves on the PTA board, has been a Girl Scout leader for six years, and loves salmon fishing ("fantastic in Alaska").

Her husband, in the wholesale business, brought home some broken boxes of crayons and one day, looking at her hoops, the wreath idea came to her.

In addition to her daughter she has two grown stepchildren.

SWEET SEASON

Here is a pleasing holiday touch, especially for a home where there are children to appreciate it, as is the case with the Rutherfords.

Holly Rutherford of Littleton, Colorado

Holly Rutherford is very busy indeed as a wife and mother of a five-year-old son and two-year-old daughter. The rest of her time goes to custom sewing for others and for her family. She particularly enjoys sewing swimwear, formal gowns, and children's apparel. She also works on her family genealogy.

TO MAKE THE WREATH

1   Some candy wrappers prevent the hot glue from adhering, so test the glue on the wrapper before constructing the wreath.

2   Arrange eight candy canes in a circle with the crooks in the center and the straight ends pointing out. Join them with a glue gun. (Work on a piece of aluminum foil to avoid getting glue on the work surface.)

3   Follow the photograph to arrange the next layer in the opposite direction, with the ends of the canes meeting; glue together.

4   Position the mints, and glue.

5   From the satin ribbon, cut sixteen 7-inch-long pieces; form into bows (see To Form a Two-Loop Bow, page 152).

6   Glue as shown in the photograph.

7   Hang the wreath from its rim.

Designer's Note
Crooked canes can be straightened by heating them on a cookie sheet in a 200° oven for three to five minutes.

SIZE
Approximately 13" diameter

BASE
Candy canes

MATERIALS AND TOOLS
16 wrapped candy canes, matched as closely as possible in shape and size
16 wrapped starlight mints
3¼ yards red satin ribbon, ⅜" wide
Aluminum foil
Glue gun

EASTER EGG ROLL

A favorite with anyone who leans to French and English country looks, this wreath should be ready to hang at the first whisper that spring is near.

Debbie Damian of River Forest, Illinois

With five sons aged two to thirteen, Debbie Damian embraces wreath-making as a nice feminine hobby. She also finds it compatible with her other hobby, gardening, as it serves "to bring the garden indoors." She likes to decorate her house with wreaths appropriate to the changing seasons.

TO MAKE THE WREATH

1 Paint each wood egg a pastel color; let dry.

2 Attach the Spanish moss to the top and sides of the grapevine wreath with the glue gun.

3 Attach a hanger to the base (see How to Hang Your Wreath, page 149).

4 Arrange the eggs around the wreath and glue them in place.

5 Handling the three ribbons as one, loop and swirl them from egg to egg around the wreath, following the photograph. Glue them under the eggs to the moss.

6 Glue a pair of ivy leaves next to each egg along with a small cluster of German statice.

7 Glue the forsythia blossoms and rosebuds on the moss, as shown in the photograph.

8 Arrange small clusters of baby's breath around the wreath, and glue.

SIZE
Approximately 17" diameter

BASE
16"-diameter grapevine wreath

MATERIALS AND TOOLS
6 wood eggs
Green Spanish moss
Dried flowers (see How to Dry Flowers and Other Naturals, page 157): clusters of baby's breath and German statice
Artificial silk flowers and leaves: 6 forsythia blossoms, 6 clusters of three 1-inch rosebuds, 6 pairs ivy leaves
Satin ribbons ⅛" wide: 2 yards each yellow, pink, and pale blue
Liquid acrylic paint: white, pink, yellow, pale blue, green
Scissors
Glue gun

BUNNY IN A BOUQUET

Spring is here! This ambitious construction presents the garden flowers and flowering branches and berries that flourish in the designer's California landscape—along with that perennial harbinger of spring, the bunny.

Debbie Darling of Bakersfield, California

Debbie Darling, with her husband's assistance, recently started her own custom floral-design business. She is especially known for her use of unusual materials—barbed wire, birds' nests, antlers, and horseshoes—in the creation of wall pieces and centerpieces, as well as wreaths.

She has always lived in Bakersfield, where her father is an architect and creative consultant and her mother is also involved in creative work. Debbie herself started training in floral design when she was fifteen, gaining skill in all the basic floriculture techniques from corsages to funeral pieces.

TO MAKE THE WREATH

1 Cut the floral wire into fifteen 5-inch lengths. Shape each into a U (like a large hairpin).

2 Before forming the kiwi vine into a wreath, prune the leaves and runners away from the vines and discard.

3 Take the four long straight pruned green vines and form an 18"-diameter round wreath base. With the pliers, twist the U-shaped wires to hold the vines together in the round.

4 To create more depth and thickness, work the clean curly pieces around the circle, intermingling one strand at a time with the base. Hold the vines together by twisting the U wires to hold. Give the wreath a shake, to make sure the vines are secure.

5 Spray the entire wreath with several light coats of Wood Tone paint and let dry.

6 Form a bow from the paper twist with two 6-inch-wide loops and two 12-inch-long streamers (see To Form a Two-Loop Bow, page 152). Glue it to the left of the wreath; weave the streamers through the vine.

7 Glue the plastic-foam block to the inner bottom curve of the wreath. For added hold, wire it to the wreath.

8 Firmly glue the bunny's bottom to the plastic foam, following the photograph.

9 Slightly break the sides of the clay pots, following the photograph.

10 To help attach the pots, shove and then glue a leftover piece of vine into each bottom hole. Put a dab of glue on the bottom of each stick and arrange the pots according to the photograph by

SIZE
Approximately 20" diameter

BASE
18"-diameter green kiwi vine wreath

MATERIALS AND TOOLS
4 straight and 15 curly long green kiwi vines
1½ yards hunter green paper twist
1¾ yards grass-green satin ribbon, ⅛" wide
Flocked bunny, 4" high
12 wooden eggs in rose, gold, and slate, 1" long
Cotton fabric pieces: 5 green, each 1½" × 4"; 1 soft rust, 2 gold and 2 orange, each 3" × 4"
Artificial silk flowers and greens: 3 tiny trailing roses and buds; stem of pale red zinnias, 3 on a stem; 5 white apple blossoms; 3 clusters of lilac; 5 mini daffodils; bunch of violets; stem of lavendar larkspur; 1-yard piece of ivy; stem of trailing strawberries; raspberries

(continued next page)

pushing the sticks into the plastic foam. Apply more glue to attach the bottoms of the pots firmly to the foam.

11 Glue Spanish moss to cover spots where any plastic foam shows.

12 Make a carrot pattern: On the cardboard, draw a carrot-shaped triangle 3⅜ inches long by 2¾ inches wide. Add a ¼-inch seam allowance all around. Cut out.

13 Draw around the carrot pattern on the back of two gold, one rust calico, and two orange pieces of fabric. Cut out.

14 Fold each triangle in half lengthwise with right sides facing; stitch both long edges together on the seam allowance line. Turn right side out. Turn in seam allowance at the top, and baste with a thread long enough to use later in gathering the top. Stuff each carrot with cotton or fiberfill.

15 Before completing the carrots, prepare carrot "greens" by making a series of narrow cuts along the wide edges of each piece of green fabric (leave about ¼ inch uncut along one edge).

16 Roll each cut green fabric strip and insert one into the top of each carrot. Pull up the basting thread to gather the carrot around the "greens" and knot the ends together.

17 Cut the satin ribbon into 8-inch lengths and tie each piece into a bow around the gathered top of each carrot (see To Form a Two-Loop Bow, page 152).

18 Glue some moss into the bottom of each clay pot. Follow the photographs to arrange and then glue the five carrots and three eggs in the larger pot, and five eggs in the smaller pot.

19 Follow the photograph to arrange and then glue on the flowers, berries, and leaves, starting at the back and working toward the front of the wreath. Stagger the height of the flower clusters, making daffodils taller and violets lower, for example. Cut the berry stems and ivy leaves into smaller lengths so they can be worked into the design.

20 Glue the remaining four eggs to the left center of the wreath.

2 clay flower pots, one 4" high × 4" wide and one 3" high × 3" wide
Small bag green Spanish moss
Small amount of fiberfill or cotton balls
Needle and thread
Plastic foam, 2" × 6" × ¾" block
Thin cardboard
Ruler
Pencil
Green floral wire
Wire cutters
Garden shears
Needlenose pliers
Scissors
Glue gun
Glossy Wood Tone Floral Spray Paint from Design Master

GIFTS OF LOVE AND
FRIENDSHIP

BEST WISHES

The Victorian influence here, enhanced with the Wedgwood blue and mauve palette, distinguishes a wreath for an office wall.

TO MAKE THE WREATH

1 Attach a hanger to the base (see How to Hang Your Wreath, page 149).

2 Lightly spray the mistletoe clusters with snow and then with glitter.

3 Following the photograph, arrange the mistletoe so it entirely covers everything except for a space of about 12 inches at the bottom of the wreath. Glue to hold.

4 Position the green and silver leaves on the mistletoe and glue.

5 From 90 inches of the rose moiré ribbon, form a bow with five 5-inch loops (two loops on one side and three on the other) and two 16-inch streamers (see To Form a French Bow, page 154). Glue the bow to the top of the wreath.

6 Starting under the bow, twist and swirl a 36-inch length of rose ribbon on the right of the wreath and a 30-inch length on the left. Glue where the ribbon touches the wreath.

SIZE
Approximately 20" diameter

BASE
18"-diameter grapevine wreath

MATERIALS AND TOOLS
(See page 94)

Connie Boyett of Bradenton, Florida

Connie Boyett likes to make wreaths for friends and undertook this special design for the office of the plastic and reconstructive surgeon for whom she works as a medical secretary. She also has a license as a nail technician, acquired while she had a daughter in college, and did sculptured nails for extra income.

MATERIALS AND TOOLS

Clusters of plastic mistletoe
(see Designer's Note
below)
Clusters of baby's breath
Bunches of ⅝" artificial
grapes: 5 rose, 4 country
blue
Pinecones: 2 large, 3
medium, 4 small
Artificial silk leaves: 14
green, 10 silver
2 small silver gift-wrapped
boxes
Moiré ribbon, 1½" wide: 4½
yards rose, 6 yards
country blue
Liquid acrylic paints: rose,
country blue
Artist's brush
Scissors
Glitter spray
Spray snow
Glue gun

7   From 3½ yards of the country blue moiré ribbon, form a bow with twelve 5-inch loops (see To Form a Florist's Bow, page 154). Cut a 20-inch length of the blue moiré ribbon for streamers. Center and wire the ribbon to the back of the bow just formed. Glue the bow on top of the rose one, so the streamers hang down.

8   As in Step 6 above, twist and swirl and glue 36- and 30-inch lengths of country blue ribbon on the wreath.

9   Arrange the grape bunches and gift boxes, as shown in the photograph, and glue in place.

10   Paint the pinecones rose and country blue. Tip the small pinecones with a spray of snow.

11   Tuck them in here and there and glue to hold.

12   Lightly glitter the baby's breath clusters and glue them on the mistletoe to add fullness.

Designer's Note

Often the costs to make a wreath can be reduced by using materials in a new way. Connie Boyett purchased an inexpensive plastic mistletoe wreath and cut it apart. She used the separate clusters as filler on her own wreath.

The individual silver leaves were once part of a large flower that she also cut apart.

FROM US IN THE U.S.A.

This small wreath of beautifully stitched hearts is the work of the designer's teenage daughter, Anni, and five of her friends, each of whom made one heart.

Carol R. Braverman of Independence, Ohio

This was a gift to an Israeli exchange student to remind her of the U.S.A. and her schoolmates in Independence, Ohio. The heart design Carol Braverman devised symbolized the love all of the girls shared for each other. Joining them in an unbroken ring spoke of their friendship. The finishing touch was a personalized message, written on the back of each heart, from each participating friend.

Designer Carol Braverman, a former home economics teacher, continues to teach various community groups. She also sells her wreaths at local crafts shows, along with topiaries and swags she has more recently developed.

TO MAKE THE WREATH

1 For the base: Curve the galvanized wire or clothes hanger into a 5-inch-diameter ring. Overlap the wire ends and wrap them with floral wire to hold.

2 Wind 1½ yards of white satin ribbon around the ring, completely covering it; glue the ends to hold.

3 To make the puffy hearts, first prepare the decorative fronts by piecing them from the three fabrics.

4 For the ¼-inch stripes on five of the hearts, cut the following strips: twenty-eight red, twenty-three muslin, and four starry blue strips, each ¾ inch wide (¼-inch seam allowances are included) by 4½ inches long.

5 **For the design on the top center heart:** Alternate five red, four starry blue, and four muslin strips, beginning and ending with the red. Pin and stitch the strips together. Press the seams open.

6 **For the design on the upper right heart:** Alternate seven red and six muslin strips, beginning and ending with the red. Pin and stitch them together. Pin and stitch a 2 by 3¾-inch piece of starry blue to the top of these stripes. Press open the seams.

7 **For the design on the lower right heart:** Alternate five red and four muslin strips, beginning and ending with the red. Pin and stitch them together. Pin and stitch a 2½ by 4½-inch rectangle of starry blue along the side of the stripes.

Cut the fabric in half across the stripes. Turn one piece around so the stripes are at opposite corners from each other. Stitch the two pieces together, matching the seams. Press open the seams.

8 **For the design on the bottom heart:** Alternate four red and three muslin strips, beginning and ending with the red. Pin and stitch them together. Pin and stitch a 2¼ by 4½-inch rectangle of starry blue along the side of the stripes. Press open the seams.

SIZE
Approximately 9" diameter

BASE
5"-diameter wire ring

MATERIALS AND TOOLS
Galvanized clothesline wire, or wire clothes hanger with hook cut off
⅛ yard each: bleached muslin, red cotton, and starry blue cotton fabrics, 45" wide
3¼ yards white satin ribbon, ⅛" wide
Fiberfill
Needle and white sewing thread
Straight pins
Scissors
Tracing paper
Transfer paper
Pencil
Floral wire
Wire cutters
Glue gun

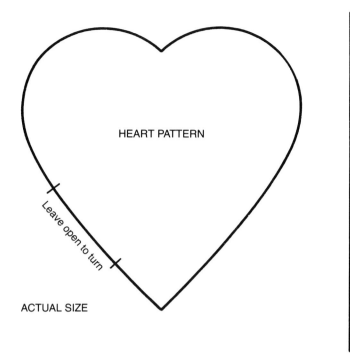

HEART PATTERN

Leave open to turn

ACTUAL SIZE

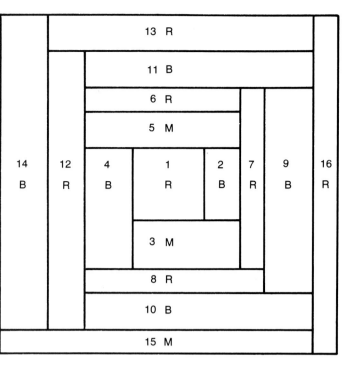

13 R							
11 B							
6 R							
5 M							
14 B	12 R	4 B	1 R	2 B	7 R	9 B	16 R
3 M							
8 R							
10 B							
15 M							

UPPER LEFT HEART

ACTUAL SIZE

R = Red fabric

B = Blue fabric

M = Muslin

9 **For the design on the lower left heart:** Alternate seven red and six muslin strips, beginning and ending with the red. Pin and stitch them together.

Cut the fabric in half across the stripes. Stitch a 1 by ¾-inch rectangle of starry blue to the two striped pieces. Press open the seams.

10 **For the design on the upper left heart:** Follow the diagram and the photograph to cut the pieces; add a ¼-inch seam allowance to each measurement.

Starting at the center square and working out, piece the fabrics together by following the numbers for the sewing order. Press open the seams.

11 For the backs: Trace the heart pattern on tracing paper, add a ¼-inch seam allowance, and transfer onto the muslin; cut out six hearts.

12 Center the muslin backs on the pieced fronts and, with right sides together, stitch around the ¼-inch seam allowance, leaving a 1-inch opening along a straight edge for turning and stuffing. Cut away excess material.

13 Turn each heart right side out. Firmly stuff all hearts with fiberfill. Hand-sew each opening closed.

14 Hand-sew the hearts together to fit the wire ring.

15 Cut the remaining satin ribbon into six even pieces and tie bows (see To Form a Two-Loop Bow, page 152) to attach the hearts to the ring.

16 Hang the wreath from its wire frame.

A HEARTFUL OF ROSES

Pink and purple and cream make a romantic palette, but note the way the designer has accented it with just a touch of yellow to give his wreath eye-catching appeal.

Charles Hardy of Sycamore, Georgia

Charles Hardy always had an interest in floral design, but until five years ago it was strictly a hobby. Then he and his wife acquired a florist shop and trained themselves in the art. The wreath took him only forty-five minutes to construct once he arrived at his design, and because his son had photographed it for him, he gave it to his daughter-in-law. The Hardys have three grown children and five grandchildren. Charles is also part-time music director at their church.

TO MAKE THE WREATH

1 For the base, form the wire or hanger into a heart shape 10 inches wide by 10 inches high (see How to Design Heart Shapes, page 155). Use the pattern as a guide to form the wire into a heart shape. Then, with needlenose pliers, crimp the ends where the wire meets.

2 Completely wrap the wire with a couple of layers of floral tape.

3 Cover the wire heart with Spanish moss, front and back, wrapping it with the finer floral wire to hold it.

4 Attach a hanger to the base (see How to Hang Your Wreath, page 149).

5 Arrange the flowers and leaves around the wreath, nestling them into the moss, as shown in the photograph.

6 Use the glue gun to attach them one by one to the Spanish moss.

7 Swirl and loop the ribbons around the wreath, gluing them here and there to hold.

Designer's Note

If Spanish moss is gathered rather than purchased, it should be treated for red bugs. Charles Hardy suggests placing it in a sealed plastic bag with a handful of mothballs for about two weeks to eliminate the bugs.

Charles cut his roses, buds, and leaves from one large branch of artificial roses.

SIZE
Approximately 13″ × 13″

BASE
10″ × 10″ wire heart

MATERIALS AND TOOLS
Galvanized clothesline wire, floral wire #20, or wire clothes hanger with hook cut off
Spanish moss
Dried statice clusters: yellow, purple, German (see How to Dry Flowers and Other Naturals, page 157)
Artificial silk roses: 5 pink, each 1¾″ wide; 4 cream, each 1¾″ wide; 8 pink rosebuds
25 each, artificial silk rose leaves and pale pink miniberry clusters
2¼ yards each, rose and mauve satin ribbon, ⅛″ wide
Floral wire
Floral tape
Wire cutters
Scissors
Needlenose pliers
Glue gun

WHITE FOR A WEDDING

This is a super idea for a wedding party centerpiece or a wall ornament for any home, contemporary, country, or traditional in decor. The wreath is made entirely with old plastic flowers from flea markets, sprayed white to give them a porcelain look.

Mary Lou Grathwohl of Niles, Michigan

"**I** am not an experienced craftsperson, but I greatly enjoy making something out of nothing, and once I get going there is nothing stopping me," says Mary Lou Grathwohl.

She made twenty-five of these wreaths as centerpieces for her oldest son's rehearsal dinner, as favors for members of the wedding party and the various shower hostesses. "The wedding colors were black and white," she reports. "So I complemented the white wreaths with black bows and placed them on beds of fresh ivy and candles."

For her youngest son's rehearsal dinner, Mary Lou and her husband made twenty-nine birdhouse centerpieces.

She works part-time as a Volunteer Coordinator at Fernwood Nature Center, Botanic Gardens and Arts and Crafts Center in Niles. The Center is growing, and so is her job. "Seldom bored," she loves to read, knit, play golf, write poems, and travel.

TO MAKE THE WREATH

1 If the straw base is covered with plastic, remove the plastic wrapping.

2 Attach a hanger to the base (see How to Hang Your Wreath, page 149).

3 With the wreath flat on a work surface, arrange the flowers and leaves around the top and sides so the larger flowers are evenly distributed. Cut stems shorter, if necessary.

4 Hold the flowers in place with the floral U-pins pushed into the wreath, and permanently attach them with the glue gun.

5 Completely spray the wreath with several coats of white paint until each flower and leaf is totally covered.

SIZE
Approximately 18" diameter

BASE
14"-diameter straw wreath

MATERIALS AND TOOLS
Plastic flowers, ½"–5" diameter, in any color (the spray paint will cover even dark-color flowers): roses, dogwood, daisies, mums, marigolds, lilac clusters
White spray paint
Floral U-pins
Garden shears
Glue gun

FOR SOMEONE SPECIAL

Roses produce some of the sweetest wreaths, and they lend a sentimental touch here. But this wreath gains a distinctive decorator look from the designer's strategic use of cedar and eucalyptus from her Nevada landscape. Indeed, she made it to blend in with her future mother-in-law's new decor.

TO MAKE THE WREATH

1 Attach a hanger to the base (see How to Hang Your Wreath, page 149).

2 Glue Spanish moss on the top and sides of the grapevine wreath for fullness and softness.

3 Position and glue the preserved cedar and eucalyptus to outline the wreath.

4 Using floral wire right under the blossoms, make approximately twenty-eight little bunches of roses, larkspur, cockscomb, German statice, and baby's breath—or enough to fill your wreath. Cut the stems very short.

5 Fill in the wreath with these little bunches of dried flowers, as shown in the photograph, hot-gluing them to hold. Use tweezers, if necessary, to push the flowers into the base.

6 Glue on cedar cones here and there.

7 From the pink ribbon, form a bow with four 1½-inch loops and four 2-inch streamers. Follow To Form a French Bow instructions, page 154, but at Step 5 bring the remaining ribbon end up, around, and under the center of the ring *twice* to form four streamers.

SIZE
Approximately 11" diameter

BASE
9"-diameter grapevine wreath

Loraine Brighton of Las Vegas, Nevada

Loraine Brighton was always out in the woods or the desert, gathering greenery and flowers, arranging them for her home. Finally her fiancé suggested she go to school and use her decorative talent to make money, so she did. She first worked in a floral shop. More recently she went into business with a friend, selling her wreaths alongside her friend's antiques and collectibles.

MATERIALS AND TOOLS

Spanish moss

Preserved cedar and eucalyptus

Cedar cones

Dried flowers (see How to Dry Flowers and Other Naturals, page 157): 18 each white and pink miniature roses, larkspur, cockscomb, German statice, baby's breath

¾ yard pink satin ribbon, ¼" wide

¾ yard mauve picot-edge satin ribbon, ⅜" wide

Floral wire

Wire cutters

Scissors

Tweezers

Glue gun

Super Surface Sealer from Design Master

8 Repeat Step 7 above to form a French bow with the mauve ribbon.

9 Glue the bow to the top of the wreath, as shown in the photograph.

10 Glue eucalyptus, cedar, and dried flowers around the bows and streamers.

11 Spray with sealer to protect the flowers.

THE KEEPSAKE
WREATH

BEADS, BUTTONS, AND BOWS

Here are ingenious ways to fashion a wall decoration from stray buttons, ribbons, and bits of jewelry.

Ruth Ratcliff rarely shops for wreath-making materials. The paper here came from a gift package, the buttons from her button box, the lace from an old tablecloth. She also makes wreaths from grapevines that grow around the ranch house in which she and her husband have lived for forty years.

Her other interests are her garden club, bridge, book reviews, a woman's club, and—of course—her daughter, son, and four grandchildren.

TO MAKE THE WREATH

1 With the compass, draw a 14-inch-diameter circle on the paneling, with a 2-inch-wide by 1½-inch-high rounded jog along the outer edge for hanging the wreath.

2 Draw an 8-inch-diameter circle in the center. With a jigsaw, cut out the inner circle and around the outer edges (see Materials and Tools, page 148). If necessary, smooth the edges with sandpaper.

3 Brush rubber cement with even strokes onto one side of the wood and onto the back of the wrapping paper. Let dry.

4 With the paper on a flat surface, glue side up, place the wood ring on it, glue side down. Lift the ring and smooth the paper with your hands. Repeat Steps 3 and 4 to finish the back of the ring.

5 Cut away all excess paper with the knife, using the wood edge of the ring as a guide.

6 Attach a hanger to the base (see How to Hang Your Wreath, page 149).

7 Hot-glue the scalloped lace, then the strung pearls, to the edges of the wreath.

8 From the wide lace ribbon, form a bow with six 3-inch loops and two 7-inch streamers (see To Form a French Bow, page 154). Hot-glue the bow to the wreath.

9 Cut nine 4-inch lengths from the narrow lace ribbon. Baste along one long edge of each length and gather into a rosette.

SIZE
Approximately 14″ diameter

BASE
14″-diameter ring made from wood paneling or Masonite

MATERIALS AND TOOLS
Wood paneling or Masonite, 18″ square
Gift wrapping paper, 2 sheets, each 18″ square
2 yards of strung pearls, approximately ³⁄₁₆″ diameter
2 yards scalloped ecru lace edging, ½″–¾″ wide
Ecru lace ribbon: 1⅜″ wide, 1⅝ yards; plus 1⅛ yards, ¾″ wide
2½ yards ecru satin ribbon, ¼″ wide
9 assorted plastic and metal buttons
11 pearls, ³⁄₁₆″ diameter
Needle and ecru thread
Pencil
Compass
Utility knife
Floral wire
Wire cutters
Scissors
Drill
Jigsaw
Rubber cement
Glue gun

Ruth W. Ratcliff
of Sunnyvale,
Texas

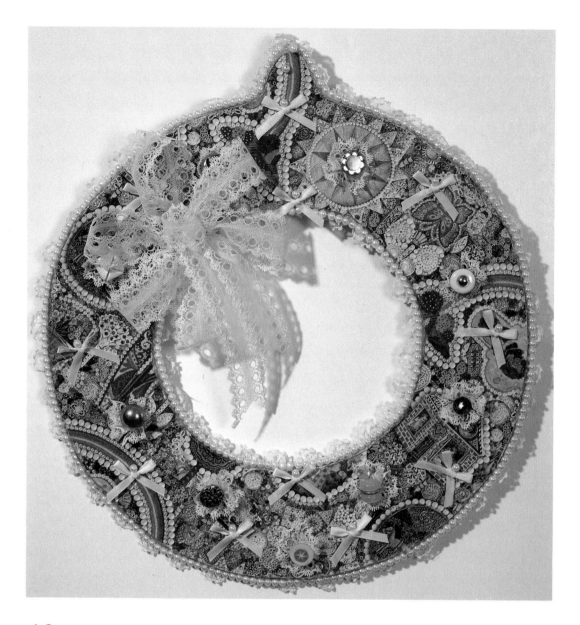

10 Cut eleven 8-inch lengths of satin ribbon and form into simple bows (see To Form a Two-Loop Ribbon, page 152). Hot-glue a button to each rosette and a pearl to each bow.

11 Glue the rosettes and bows on the wreath, spacing them as in the photograph.

TO REMEMBER THE DAY

Here's a way to showcase Christmas memorabilia or, as the designer suggests, to create conversation pieces celebrating a new baby, a teenage birthday, or Mother's Day with decorative elements appropriate to the people involved.

Patricia Pritchett of Alviso, California

Patricia Pritchett, now single, with a grown son and a new daughter-in-law, works as a cook for the county Department of Corrections. In addition to designing wreaths, she decorates recycled straw hats with silk flowers and creates miniature scenes on burl wood.

TO MAKE THE WREATH

1   For the base: With the compass draw an 18-inch circle on the wood paneling or Masonite. Draw an 8-inch circle in the center.

2   Cut around the inner and outer circles with the jigsaw (see Materials and Tools, page 148).

3   If necessary, smooth all the edges with sandpaper.

4   Attach a hanger to the base (see How to Hang Your Wreath, page 149).

5   If there are not enough gift boxes to cover the base completely, cut extra box shapes from the wood, using the jigsaw, or from the plastic foam, using the serrated knife.

SIZE
Approximately 20" diameter

BASE
18"-diameter ring of wood paneling or Masonite

6 To fill the empty edges along the rim of the circle, cut triangular "boxes" of plastic foam with the serrated knife.

7 Wrap all boxes, including the fake ones, in the printed papers, securing them with adhesive tape.

8 Position the first layer of boxes on the wood ring and, with the glue gun, attach them one by one.

9 Now hang the wreath on the wall or other vertical surface to work on it. Starting at the bottom, begin gluing on more boxes to act as ledges for the objects to rest on. Arrange and then glue some objects on these ledges.

10 Continue placing boxes to create more ledges, attaching them with the glue gun until the wreath is covered. Hot-glue more objects on and around the boxes. ("The wreath is complete," says the designer, "when you decide it is wonderful.")

11 Form small bows from the 12-inch ribbon pieces (see To Form a Two-Loop Bow, page 152), and glue on randomly.

MATERIALS AND TOOLS
Wood paneling or Masonite, 19" square
Small gift boxes, cardboard containers (new or recycled) or pieces of wood or plastic-foam sheets cut into small blocks ½"–5" long
Small decorative fabric, wood, plastic, or metal objects, such as baby blocks, train, drum, banjo, teddy bear, heart, cards, wagon, 1"–5" high
Scraps of gift wrap and other printed papers (new or leftovers)
Assorted ribbon, 12"-long pieces
Adhesive tape
Compass
Tweezers (optional, for handling small items)
Serrated kitchen knife
Scissors
Medium sandpaper
Drill
Jigsaw
Glue gun

PLEASANT PASTIME

Here's a great way to create memories: Just make a wreath with the little bits and pieces that remind you of your favorite hobbies and connections. This designer's loves are family, sewing, and cooking.

Sylvia Dollina of Orange, California

Married thirty-three years and the mother of two children, Sylvia has also owned a vending business for ten years. She considers herself "very independent," declaring that "creativity is *not* following a basic pattern. Let your imagination go!"

TO MAKE THE WREATH

1 If the straw base is wrapped in plastic, remove the plastic wrapping.

2 Attach a hanger to the base (see How to Hang Your Wreath, page 149).

3 Spray all the fabrics with Scotch-gard; let dry.

4 Next, working on the back of each of the fabrics, mark off with the ruler a series of 3-inch squares—about 588 in all. Carefully cut the squares with the pinking shears.

5 Center the Phillips screwdriver in the middle of each square and push it into the straw base, giving the square a puckered look. Continue until you have covered the entire top and sides of the wreath, and the squares are used up.

6 Starting at the end of one of the measuring tapes, form a series of eight even loops, each about 3½ inches long. Attach this loop cluster to the lower right side of the wreath with long straight pins.

7 In the center of the second tape, form a 2-inch loop; position it in the middle of the previously formed loop cluster, and pin it to the base with long straight pins. Swirl the tape ends to the left across the bottom of the wreath. Hot-glue to hold in place.

8 Open the scissors and press their pointed ends into the wreath, as shown in the photograph. Insert the screws into the spool openings and screw into the base.

9 Paint the tomato and strawberry pincushion with the blue acrylic paint. Let dry and hot-glue to attach.

SIZE
Approximately 25" diameter

BASE
24"-diameter straw wreath

MATERIALS AND TOOLS
7½ yards cotton fabric, 45" wide, in solids, calicos, and small prints in shades of rose, slate blue, ecru
2 measuring tapes, each 60" long
Pink-handled scissors, 6" long
5 spools sewing thread in shades of rose and blue
"Tomato" fabric pincushion with hanging strawberry
5 painted 2" screws, to fit spool openings
Ruler
Pencil
Long straight pins (bank pins)
Pinking shears
Screwdrivers: Phillips, regular
Slate blue liquid acrylic paint
Artist's brush
Glue gun
Scotch-gard Fabric Protector

Designer's Note
Sylvia Dollina made this wreath to match a quilt in her sewing room. But she has made similar wreaths for kitchens and bedrooms and for Christmas. "They can be made for any room and any occasion," she says, "and with small stuffed animals and miniatures of any kind."

THE GREAT-GRANDMA WREATH

Here is a superb example of the "keepsake wreath," a great way to display personal and family treasures.

TO MAKE THE WREATH

1 Wind the 11 yards of velvet craft ribbon around the wire form until the form is completely covered. Glue ends to hold. If the surface is not soft enough to act as a base for the mementos, wind a second layer over the first.

2 Attach a hanger to the base (see How to Hang Your Wreath, page 149).

3 To make a pair of double ruffles to frame both the front and back of the wreath, start by cutting the two ruffled laces in half, to make four equal lengths. Join a narrow length to a wider one along the straight unruffled edge by sewing them by hand or machine, using a narrow zigzag stitch. Complete the second double ruffle in the same manner.

4 Follow the contour of the wreath to glue a double ruffle on one side with the narrow lace following the inner circle. Do the same with the second ruffle on the reverse side. (The 2½-inch-wide lace follows the inner circle.) Begin and end both pieces of lace in the same place on the wreath.

5 Pick one side to be the front of the wreath and glue the dried flower cluster at the place where the lace begins and ends.

6 Form the satin ribbon into a series of three 6-inch loops and four 2-inch loops; wire them together. Glue next to the flower cluster.

7 Position the memorabilia around the wreath on the front with some emerging from the back also.

8 If the mementos are to be put on permanently, use a glue gun to attach them one by one; otherwise, sew the objects on with needle and thread.

SIZE
Approximately 20″ diameter

BASE
16″-diameter wire wreath form

MATERIALS AND TOOLS
11 (or 22) yards white velvet craft ribbon, 1⁷⁄₁₆″ wide (see Step 1)
3½ yards each, ruffled white lace 3½″ wide and 2½″ wide
1¾ yards mauve satin ribbon, ¼″ wide
Dried flowers (see How to Dry Flowers and Other Naturals, page 157): 5″ cluster of pink baby roses and white skyrockets
Memorabilia: 5½″ china doll, spectacles, sewing scissors, key, thimbles, threads on spools and in packages, tatting shuttle, bone crochet hook, turn-of-the-century thermometer, crocheted gloves, piece of knitted lace on needles, Victorian postcard
Needle and white thread
Scissors
Glue gun

LoRae Pursian of Coos Bay, Oregon

"**W**e have been the fortunate recipients of many of our family's mothers', grandmothers', and great-grandmothers' sewing notions, including unfinished lace still on the knitting needle," says LoRae Pursian, "and reading about the wreath contest jogged something in my mind." It inspired her to showcase them in a wreath.

LoRae has been a crafter since childhood. She has always taken her husband and children to museums to enjoy the beauty in objects handmade by people throughout the centuries. Now she has settled on wreaths and porcelain dolls as her favorites to make, and with her children grown and on their own, she plans to go into these crafts professionally.

IN LOVE WITH ANOTHER ERA

This evokes the rustic charm of another scene and another century: nineteenth-century Germany. Wreaths are a perfect medium, says this designer, because they allow a choice among so many different materials with different colors, textures, and connotations. Other wreaths of hers have featured cherubs and teddy bears.

Charlene Geiger of Danville, California

The inspiration for Charlene Geiger's wreath, the clay hare, is a replica of a nineteenth-century hand-carving. She felt a wonderful way to display this lovable bunny with its broken ear was to nestle it in a floral wreath.

Charlene became involved with wreath-making by accident. She went to a warehouse auction in 1985 to buy a typewriter and ended up buying the type-writer—but also 1,000 grapevine wreaths. "My husband said either to start creating, or the vines would make great firewood." So she taught herself to make wreaths, burying some first attempts in the backyard.

She now teaches the art occasionally at local garden clubs and does floral design for a decorator gallery and an English garden shop, Capability Brown.

She has been married fifteen years and has three children, Haley and Reid and a new baby born after the contest just as this book was written. She provides floral pieces for Down's Syndrome League benefit auctions. Her son has Down's syndrome, and in creating her floral design business it is her hope to make a place for him to work when he grows up, if he so chooses.

She has other art-related hobbies and loves outdoor activities of all sorts. (Except gardening: "Boy do I have one brown thumb!")

TO MAKE THE WREATH

1 Circle the grapevine or willow branches in the wire wreath form until it is completely filled. If the branches are stiff, first dampen them.

2 Wrap wire around the form to hold the branches in place securely.

3 Attach a hanger to the base (see How to Hang Your Wreath, page 149).

4 Stand the rabbit head on the corrugated cardboard; trace around its base and cut out the resulting shape. Use a large pin to make two holes in the center of the cardboard.

5 Cut a 15-inch length of wire and work it through the holes in the cardboard, leaving two long ends hanging on one side.

6 Hot-glue this cardboard base to the base of the rabbit so the wire ends are on the outside.

7 Position the rabbit head to the top front of the wreath; wrap the wire ends from the cardboard base around the wreath and twist them to hold the head firmly.

SIZE
Approximately 20″ diameter

BASE
14″-diameter double wire
   wreath form

MATERIALS AND TOOLS
(See page 118)

8 Before proceeding further, have all the flowers and materials prepared and laid out ready for use.

9 Lightly dust the hydrangea clusters with three colors of spray (to give them a natural look).

10 Dip the millet, lace, and edgings into acrylic paint thinned with water (use any of the colors indicated); shake out excess and let dry.

11 Glue a foundation of sprayed hydrangea clusters to the wreath base so that the rabbit appears to be nestled in the flowers.

12 Follow the photograph to position and then glue the remaining flowers. If the wreath seems thin, add more layers of flowers.

13 Glue in the bits of colored lace and edgings randomly.

14 Attach the rosebud potpourri throughout the wreath by using the glue gun here and there; before the glue dries, sprinkle on the potpourri and later shake out the excess.

15 Form the wire-edge taffeta ribbon into a bow with two 9-inch loops and two 9-inch streamers (see To Form a Two-Loop Bow, page 152).

16 Glue the wire-edge taffeta bow just below the rabbit's head, tucked into the flowers. Use the heated hair crimper to crimp the ribbon, as shown in the photograph.

Designer's Note

Charlene Geiger's garage ceiling is covered with the hanging floral material she has gathered from season to season. Close family members and friends often send her materials native to their area. Whenever she sees a yard full of hydrangeas, she makes a wreath, basket, or door swag to barter for them.

To cope with burns when working with a glue gun, she keeps a bowl of ice handy to dip her fingers into when she gets a little careless.

MATERIALS AND TOOLS

Fresh grapevine or willow branches
Flowers to be dried by the silica-gel method (see How to Dry Flowers and Other Naturals, page 157): hydrangeas separated into clusters, roses, strawflowers, baby's breath, Sweet Annie, millet
Scented rosebud potpourri
Clay rabbit head, approximately 6″ high
1¾ yards gray-green wire-edge taffeta ribbon, 1½″ wide
Scraps of laces and braids
Scrap of corrugated cardboard
Colored matte sprays and liquid acrylic paints: teal, lavender, Wedgwood blue
Floral wire
Wire cutters
Scissors
Hair crimper
Glue gun

SENTIMENTAL
JOURNEYS TO A
GENTLER TIME

NOSTALGIA IN TULLE

Jeanne Brackin of Gulfport, Mississippi

TO MAKE THE WREATH

1 Wind the moiré craft ribbon around the plastic-foam base until the base is completely covered. Glue ends to hold.

2 Attach a hanger to the base (see How To Hang Your Wreath, page 149).

3 See How to Form Bows, pages 151–155, to make the following bows:

4 Cut the velvet craft ribbon into eight 1-yard lengths and form eight French bows, each with six 2-inch loops and two 4-inch streamers.

5 Cut the picot-edge satin ribbon into 18-inch lengths and form seven two-loop bows, each with two 1½-inch loops and two 5-inch streamers.

6 Cut the satin ribbon into nine 12-inch lengths and form nine two-loop bows, each with two 1-inch loops and two 3-inch-long streamers.

7 Cut the scalloped lace ribbon into fourteen 1-yard lengths and form fourteen French bows, each with four 3-inch loops and two 4-inch-long streamers.

8 Cut the lace ribbon into five ¾-yard lengths and form five two-loop bows each with two 3-inch loops and two 6-inch streamers.

9 Cut the tulle into five 1-yard pieces and form into six 2¾-inch loops. Wire loops together to hold.

10 Glue the tulle bows around the wreath.

11 Form little flower bunches by adding a few globe amaranth to each cluster of baby's breath. Place one little flower bunch in the center of each doily. Twist the doily around the flowers to form a rosette.

12 Arrange and then glue these flower and doily rosettes in the tulle, spacing them around the wreath.

13 Glue the bows around the wreath, layering ribbon on tulle, on other ribbons, on doilies, and around the flower and doily rosettes.

14 Loop, swirl, and glue the pearls around the wreath.

SIZE
Approximately 20″ diameter

BASE
16″-diameter plastic-foam wreath

MATERIALS AND TOOLS
Note: All ribbons, lace, tulle, doilies, and feathers are cream-colored
10 yards moiré craft ribbon, 1¾″ wide
8 yards velvet craft ribbon, ⅝″ wide
3¾ yards picot-edge satin ribbon, ⅜″ wide
3⅛ yards satin ribbon, ⅛″ wide
14 yards scalloped lace ribbon, ¾″ wide
4 yards lace ribbon, ⅛″ wide
5¼ yards soft nylon tulle ribbon, 6″ wide
12 round paper doilies, 4″ diameter
1½ yards strung pearls
Soft feathers
Dried flowers (see How to Dry Flowers and Other Naturals, page 157): globe amaranth and 3″ clusters of baby's breath
Glue gun

This confection belongs in a home with a Victorian aura, but the design could also be gorgeous in pinks or mauves or make a fabulous Christmas accent if done in ecru and gold.

Jeanne Brackin designed this when she was in the midst of planning her wedding and busily designing hats, dresses, and flowers for that event. Ribbons and laces were on her mind. In any case, Jeanne says, "I am a hopeless romantic. I often wonder if I belong to the Victorian era."

She wishes she could spend more time on wreath design, but she holds a full-time job as an account executive with United Parcel Service and has three children now—one of her own and two from her new husband's previous marriage. She hopes she'll someday find a way to work at home on wreath design and be a "housewife," when school lets out.

LACY SENTIMENT

This was a Mother's Day gift, but it could convey love to anyone or serve as an accent in any room with Victorian touches.

Nancy F. Smith of Centerville, Utah

Nancy Smith grew up in a small farming community where there were no stores carrying crafts materials. But her artistic parents taught her to work with wood, and she learned to make her own crafts items of all kinds.

Since making this wreath for her mother, she has duplicated it for her sisters and has also sold some.

Married, with two sons and a daughter, she is a busy homemaker occupied with cooking and sewing, putting on a Christmas boutique at home each year, and sending other crafts items to stores and boutiques in other states.

TO MAKE THE WREATH

1 For the base, draw a heart 7 inches wide by 5 inches high on the cardboard (see How to Design Heart Shapes, page 155).

2 Draw a second heart in the center of the first, allowing for a ¾-inch border all around. Use the utility knife to cut out the heart frame.

3 Completely wrap the frame with the Pellon or nylon net strips, by winding them around and gluing the ends to hold.

4 Attach a hanger to the base (see How to Hang Your Wreath, page 149).

5 With the wreath base face-down on a flat surface, start at the top where the heart dips down, to arrange and then glue the gathered lace on the back, following the heart edge; overlap the ends.

6 For the 1-inch roses, cut the ¾-inch-wide satin ribbons into ¾-yard lengths. This will produce seven peach and three rose-colored roses.

7 For the ½-inch roses, cut the ¼-inch satin ribbons into 15-inch lengths, producing seven deep rose, six pink, six teal, and four yellow flowers.

8 Before forming the roses, cut thirty-three 3-inch lengths of floral wire and set aside.

9 Make thirty-three folded ribbon roses (see How to Make Folded Ribbon Roses, page 124). (**Note:** Forming these roses can be a little tricky and may require some practice, so you may want to have some extra satin ribbon on hand.)

10 Follow the photograph to position the 1-inch roses; hot-glue.

11 Position and hot-glue the ½-inch roses, using tweezers to handle them, if necessary.

SIZE
Approximately 10″ wide × 9″ high

BASE
Cardboard heart, 7″ wide × 5″ high

MATERIALS AND TOOLS
Corrugated cardboard or foamcore, 6″ × 8″
1 yard gathered ecru lace, 2½″ wide
Satin ribbon, ¼″ wide: 3 yards deep rose; 2¾ yards pink; 2¾ yards teal; 1¾ yards yellow
Satin ribbon, ¾″ wide: 5½ yards peach, 2½ yards rose
12 yards pink satin ribbon, ⅝″ wide
German statice
7 artificial silk asters, ½″ wide: turquoise, rose, yellow
2 yards Pellon or nylon net, ½″ wide
Floral wire
Wire cutters
Utility knife
Tweezers
Corsage pin
Glue gun

12 Glue on the silk flowers.

13 From the ⅝-inch-wide pink ribbon, cut sixty 7-inch lengths and form bows with two 1-inch-long loops and two 1-inch-long streamers (see To Form a Two-Loop Bow, page 152). Wrap wire around the middle of each bow to hold.

14 Fill the wreath with the pink ribbon loops, using a corsage pin to help poke them down into the wreath and to hold them in place until the glue dries.

15 Accent the wreath by gluing small pieces of German statice here and there throughout.

HOW TO MAKE FOLDED RIBBON ROSES

1 To form the roses, fold the ribbon in the middle so the tails are at right angles to each other (see Figure 1).

2 Fold the right tail over around the back and to the left (see Figure 2).

3 Fold the bottom tail over the back and up (see Figure 3).

4 Fold the left tail over, around the back and to the right (see Figure 4).

5 Fold the top tail over the back and down (see Figure 5).

6 Continue following Steps 2 through 5 until the tails are ¾ to 1 inch long and one is facing right and the other is facing down.

7 Slip left thumb into the top pocket and, with the left index finger behind, gently hold folds while pulling the right tail to the right with the right hand until the desired rose is formed (see Figure 6).

8 Hold the tails together and wrap them with floral wire.

FOLDED RIBBON ROSES

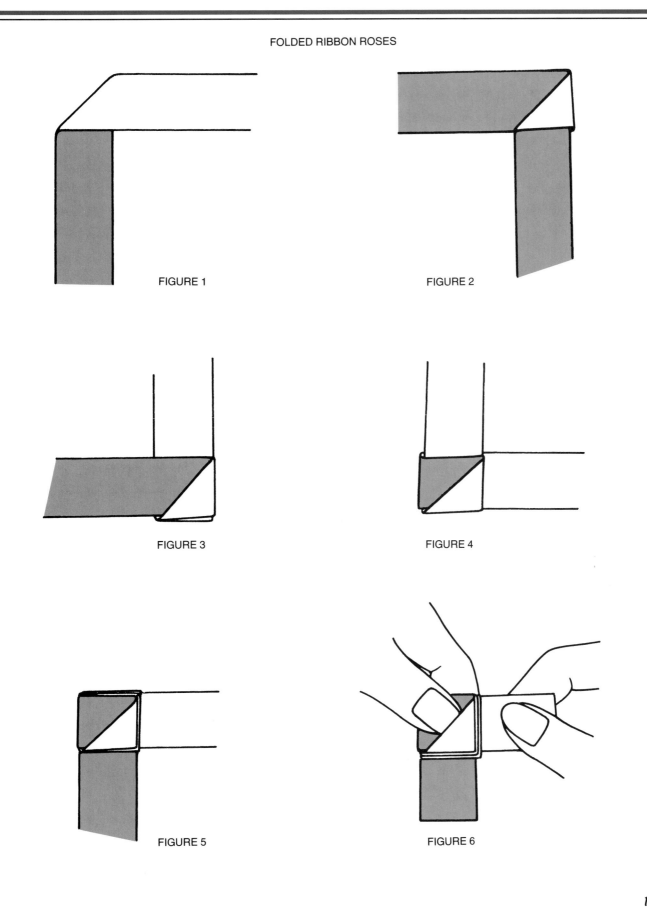

FIGURE 1

FIGURE 2

FIGURE 3

FIGURE 4

FIGURE 5

FIGURE 6

VICTORIAN GRACE

Pale pink, dusty rose, miniature ornaments, lace-banded ribbon, "antiqued" music sheets—these all transform a round of artificial greenery into a celebration of Victorian taste.

TO MAKE THE WREATH

1 Attach a hanger to the base (see How to Hang Your Wreath, page 149).

2 Cut 2¼ yards each from the lace and grosgrain ribbons. Center the grosgrain behind the lace and form a bow with eight 4½-inch loops (see To Form a Starburst Bow, page 152).

3 Glue the bow to the base.

4 Swirl the remaining ribbon-backed lace around the wreath, gluing the ends under the bow and wherever it touches the wreath.

5 Follow the photograph to wire and glue the musical instruments on the wreath.

6 Carefully burn the edges of the sheet music over a lighted match, to give them an antique appearance, blowing out the flame if it seems to be going beyond the edges.

7 Glue the sheet music on top of the lace, as shown in the photograph.

8 Secure the four bunches of berries to the wreath with glue.

9 Position and glue the baby's breath clusters here and there on the wreath.

10 Finally, insert and glue the heather stems so they radiate out from the edge of the wreath.

SIZE
Approximately 27" diameter

BASE
18"-diameter artificial pine wreath

MATERIALS AND TOOLS
4 yards ecru lace, 2¾" wide
4 yards mauve grosgrain ribbon, ⅞" wide
Christmas sheet music, 2 pieces 6" × 8"
3 miniature musical instruments, 6" high: tuba, 2 violins
Dried flowers (see How to Dry Flowers and Other Naturals, page 157): baby's breath clusters, pink and white heather
4 bunches artificial pink berries with leaves
Floral wire
Wire cutters
Glue gun

Patrice Scholtes-Hightower of Menlo Park, California

Patrice Scholtes-Hightower started with crafts and sewing at an early age, guided by an artistic mother, and grew up designing and creating costumes, decorations, and gifts for Christmas, Halloween, and other holidays.

Then, for a while, as the General Manager of a busy historical landmark restaurant and bar, she found little time for crafts work. It wasn't until she married, in 1984, that she left the restaurant business and began a small, part-time crafts operation out of her home. As her crafts work grew in popularity, she branched out into other areas, including specialty wreaths and a line of toddler boys' wear, named for her active two-year-old son: Collinville Station.

She says this particular Victorian wreath is her favorite—not to mention her very best seller!

SWEET MINIATURE

This adorable little wreath, shown actual size, is appropriate for a wedding, Valentine's Day, an anniversary, or, as the designer says, "any year-round event."

Ruby Yagoobian of West Bloomfield, Michigan

"**A**s long as I can remember," says Ruby Yagoobian, "I have taken classes in china painting, weaving, drawing, and watercolor painting. I enjoy doing everything!"

Ruby has been married more than forty years "to a wonderful husband who is now a retired physician." Two children and two grandchildren complete the family.

TO MAKE THE WREATH

1 Draw a heart 5½ inches wide by 5½ inches high (see How to Design Heart Shapes, page 155).

2 Form the heart-shaped base, following this pattern, using one strand of the heavy-gauge wire, bending it by hand, and using the pliers to crimp the wire together where the ends meet.

3 Completely cover the base with strands of artemisia, attaching them strand by strand, anchoring the ends with green floral tape. Curve each piece to follow the heart shape, and wrap with the lightweight wire to secure.

4 Attach a hanger to the base (see How to Hang Your Wreath, page 149).

5 With the glue gun, using tweezers where helpful, attach small pieces of statice, baby's breath, fern, and the rose leaves until the wreath is layered and full.

6 Position the roses and violas, as shown in the photograph; attach them with the glue gun.

7 To make ten satin roses, cut the ⅜-inch-wide ribbon into ten 5-inch lengths. Also thread the needle and set aside.

8 Cut one end of each length of ribbon on the diagonal and start rolling it between thumb and fingers very tightly, from the center out. About halfway, fold the ribbon in half lengthwise and continue rolling it. To hold the ribbon end to the ribbon layers, take a few stitches through the bottom of the rose. Make nine more roses in the same way.

9 With glue gun, join seven of these roses to form a cluster. Attach the cluster and the three remaining roses to the wreath with the glue gun, as shown in the photograph.

10 Rip the pink and purple curling ribbon into eight ½₂-inch-wide strips. Curl strips on a blade of the scissors and glue them at random into the wreath.

SIZE
Approximately 6" × 6"

BASE
A heart 5½" wide × 5½" high, shaped from heavy-gauge green floral wire

MATERIALS AND TOOLS
Spool of heavy-gauge green floral wire
Silica-gel-dried flowers and leaves (see How to Dry Flowers and Other Naturals, page 157): baby roses and leaves, violas, purple and yellow statice, baby's breath (white and pale green), fern
Fresh artemisia
Rose satin ribbon, ⅜" wide, 1½ yards; ⅛" wide, 1 yard
½ yard each pink and purple paper curling ribbon, ½" wide
Needle and rose thread
Green floral tape
Lightweight floral wire
Wire cutters
Needlenose pliers
Tweezers
Glue gun

11   With the ⅛-inch-wide satin ribbon, form a bow with five 1-inch loops and two 7-inch streamers (see To Form a French Bow, page 154). Glue in place above the rose cluster; loop and swirl the ribbon ends into the wreath as shown and hot-glue in place.

Designer's Note

Because Ruby Yagoobian's wreath is so tiny, she chose miniature flowers to keep the trimmings in scale, and because the flowers are so small, she uses tweezers to handle them.

You might use her method to make larger wreaths, with silk flowers instead of dried.

KEEPING THE
CHRISTMAS TRADITION

APPLES AT THE HEARTH

A cheerful "Welcome home!" any time of year, this wreath is also a special celebration of the Christmas season at this designer's house.

Judie L. Bennett of Fort Hood, Texas

"I have been married for eight years and have three super children," says Judie Bennett. "I have a crafts business, which I run out of my house. I have done local crafts shows, given demonstrations for military wives [the Bennetts are a military family], and sold items on consignment at area crafts stores. My business has been in operation for three years. However, I still consider it more of a hobby.

"I don't have a workroom, so all the flowers and wreaths are pulled out of the closet and put on the kitchen sink. I usually work while my two oldest children are in school or after they go to bed. The few weeks prior to crafts shows I usually get very little sleep and my house looks like a display room. All my inventory is up on the walls to keep the children from attacking it."

TO MAKE THE WREATH

1 Attach a hanger to the base (see How to Hang Your Wreath, page 149).

2 Cut a 50-inch length from the ribbon. Roll and twirl it along the lower half of the wreath, as shown in the photograph, and attach it firmly with the glue gun.

3 Cut the remaining ribbon into two lengths, 54 inches and 28 inches.

4 From the 54-inch length form a bow with six 3-inch loops and two 7-inch streamers (see To Form a French Bow, page 154).

5 From the 28-inch length form a bow with two 3-inch loops and two 7-inch streamers (see To Form a Two-Loop Bow, page 152).

6 Wire the two-loop bow to the top of the six-loop bow and top it with a 3-inch wired-on round of ribbon (see To Form a Ribbon Round, page 151).

7 Wire the bow to the top of the wreath.

8 Position the apples around the wreath; glue them in place one by one.

9 Arrange clusters of skyrockets, eucalyptus, and statice around the apples and the ribbon; glue in place. If necessary, first wrap the flower stems with floral tape right under the blossoms, and then cut the stems short before gluing the clusters into the wreath.

SIZE
Approximately 24" diameter

BASE
24"-diameter artificial pine wreath

MATERIALS AND TOOLS
12 plastic apples, 3" diameter
14 pieces green eucalyptus, 6" long
Dried flowers (see How to Dry Flowers and Other Naturals, page 157): 12 small clusters red skyrockets, German statice
4 yards Christmas plaid taffeta ribbon, 2¾" wide
Floral tape
Scissors
Floral wire
Wire cutters
Glue gun

SILVER CIRCLE

This silver-and-white fantasy, when hung on a brown door like the Kenneys', sparkles like new snow. (It could be the way to have a white Christmas wherever you live!)

TO MAKE THE WREATH

1 Attach a hanger to the base (see How to Hang Your Wreath, page 149).

2 If the natural materials are not already painted, spray the grapevine wreath and half of the twigs and grasses white, and the remaining twigs and grasses silver. Let dry.

3 Mix the silver and white twigs and grasses and make two clusters. Wire one cluster to the right and another to the left of the top of the wreath, as shown in the photograph.

4 Wire on the berry sprays so they cascade down each side of the wreath.

5 With 6¾ yards of the ribbon, form a bow with twenty 6-inch loops (see To Form a Florist's Bow, page 154).

6 Cut five 16-inch lengths from the remaining ribbon for streamers. Center and wire the streamers to the back of the bow so they fan out on both sides, as seen in the photograph.

7 Hot-glue a 2-inch ribbon round to the center of the bow (see To Form a Ribbon Round, page 151).

8 Glue the bow securely to the top center of the wreath.

9 Arrange the holly leaf clusters and mini poinsettias around the bow, and glue.

Designer's Note

Melinda Kenney always takes into consideration where her wreaths will be displayed before she makes them. On a windy west-facing location, she uses wire as well as glue to hold the materials in place. If it's a humid area, she uses scented materials like cloves or cinnamon because the dampness brings out the fragrance.

SIZE
Approximately 16" diameter

BASE
16"-diameter grapevine wreath sprayed white

MATERIALS AND TOOLS
4 berry sprays, 12" long: 2 gray, 2 white pearl
3 silver holly-leaf clusters with pearl berries
4 clusters of silver mini poinsettias
Clusters of fine twigs and grasses sprayed white and silver, 2 each
9¼ yards silvery metallic plaid ribbon, 1⅜" wide
Floral wire
Wire cutters
Garden shears
Scissors
Glue gun
Spray paints: matte white, silver (optional)

Melinda A. Kenney of Lindenhurst, Illinois

Melinda Kenney's note about herself was topped with a letterhead, *Design Vine. Custom Made Wall and Door Designs.* This part-time venture is especially suited to Melinda's life, which revolves around two small boys, aged five and seven, and includes activity in the local Newcomers Club, her children's school, and her church. "And because every wreath is different, I get to satisfy my creative urges at a profit!"

Melinda says she has more wreath ideas than she has time or money for, but she tries to make each wreath one of a kind. She uses bells and scented flowers on her wreaths and includes the meanings of the flowers and herbs adorning them.

CHRISTMAS IS A BALL

Here is a wreath that seems to shout "Christmas," whether it's lighted or just reflecting the daytime scene.

Phyllis Hovenden of Thomasville, North Carolina

Hands-on projects have always been a love of Phyllis Hovenden's. "I have owned my own crafts shop, worked as a floral designer and freelance interior designer." Her husband, Bill, is an educational consultant; her son is a kindergartener.

Her wreath-making didn't begin until after she quit her floral design work and had her son, when she and a friend decided to stage a "Holiday House" and sell Christmas wreaths and arrangements.

She has now made hundreds of wreaths and has had two shows.

TO MAKE THE WREATH

1 Attach a hanger to the base (see How to Hang Your Wreath, page 149).

2 Evenly space the largest Christmas balls around the wreath. With the glue gun, attach them firmly one by one.

3 Continue with the medium balls, and then the small ones.

4 Arrange small clumps of baby's breath on the wreath; glue in place one by one.

5 Cut and then weave 8 yards of the fabric tubing around the Christmas balls, rippling and looping it. Glue each loop to the wreath. (**Note:** The tubing is easier to handle if it's first cut into shorter 1-yard lengths. Just be sure to bury the ends in the wreath so the tubing looks like one continuous strand.)

6 Cut the remaining tubing into 10- and 14-inch lengths and firmly glue into the side of the wreath, as shown in the photograph.

7 Glue a larger ball to the short end and a small ball to the long end. Glue a sprig of artificial pine (taken from the back of the wreath), and a cluster of baby's breath to the top of each Christmas ball.

SIZE
Approximately 20" diameter

BASE
20"-diameter artificial pine wreath

MATERIALS AND TOOLS
Glass Christmas balls in gold, red, green, royal, silver: 20, each 1"; 19, each 1½"; 21, each 2"
9 yards gold metallic fabric tubing
Preserved baby's breath clusters
Scissors
Floral wire
Wire cutters
Glue gun

JUST RIBBONS

This wreath works well in many decorative schemes. It's simple, but ever so elegant.

Jill M. Oleksy of Middleburg Heights, Ohio

Jill Oleksy prided herself on making gifts "too pretty to open." Then she discovered "a whole world of ribbon out there that has nothing to do with gift-wrapping. I was instantly addicted!"

She has used up to ten different patterns of ribbon in one wreath, and as few as one. Her winner is her fifth design. Her favorite is one that grew to a giant 24 inches in diameter, made for her brother but too big to ship to him in Hawaii.

Jill started making things at a very young age: everything from embroidered pillows to sequined Christmas ornaments to three-piece suits when she started her first job after high school. Now a "stay-at-home Mom," she is building an inventory of wreaths to start a crafts business of her own.

TO MAKE THE WREATH

1 Attach a hanger to the base (see How to Hang Your Wreath, page 149).

2 Cut the ribbons into 30-inch lengths.

3 Place the straw wreath flat on a work surface. Now, one at a time, from each ribbon length, make a series of bows with four 3½-inch loops. (See To Form a Florist's Bow, page 154. However, repeat Steps 1 and 2 just until four loops are formed, and omit Steps 3 and 4.)

4 Holding the loops together, insert a U-pin around their middle and press the pin firmly into the wreath. (**Note:** A leather-sewer's thimble worn on the thumb can be helpful in pushing in the pins.) Place the bows on the inner and outer edges of the wreath first so they are parallel to the work surface.

5 Continue to form four-loop bows until the wreath is covered, pushing them into the wreath at various angles and arranging them so the color and pattern are well mixed.

SIZE
Approximately 18″ diameter

BASE
12″-diameter straw wreath

MATERIALS AND TOOLS
Taffeta ribbon, 1⅜″ wide: 50 yards red-and-green plaid; 35 yards red
Floral U-pins, approximately 102
Scissors
Leather sewer's thimble (optional)
Scotch-gard Fabric Protector

6 If you wish, spray the wreath with Scotch-gard Fabric Protector.

Designer's Note

Although this design was created with Christmas in mind, it can be changed to suit any decor or to celebrate any holiday simply by changing the color or pattern of the ribbons.

As for the base, it requires no preparation. If it comes wrapped in plastic, leave the plastic on, as it holds the straw in place. If the wreath will hang in a window where its base shows, wrap it first in an additional 10 to 11 yards of the ribbon being used.

When selecting ribbon, acetate is the easiest to work with. Craft ribbon, on the other hand, is often stiff and difficult to handle, but it comes in a wide variety of designs and patterns.

Five yards of ribbon will make six bows. When using different ribbons, buy them in multiples of 5 yards to eliminate waste.

JEWELED STAR

Anyone who loves to comb through flea markets and yard sales will enjoy making this wreath. And it could well provide a showcase for some bits of your own jewelry that have sifted to the bottom of the jewel box.

Mary Ellen Chronister
of Greenbrae, California

Mary Ellen Chronister works at the Federal Reserve Bank of San Francisco and makes dolls for their United Way auction. She has been married eleven years, with a married stepdaughter for whom she sewed and beaded the roller skating costumes she wore in competition as a teenager. Mary Ellen is the guardian of a retarded sister and crochets hats and scarves as money-raisers for the church program for the handicapped in which her sister participates. For ten years she has attended evening classes to get her A.S. degree in Small Business Management—in the hope that that knowledge plus her crafts skills will enable her to start a small arts-and-crafts business.

TO MAKE THE WREATH

1   To make the star base, follow the diagram, using a ruler and pencil to draw lines from corner to corner of the plywood square. Divide each plywood edge in half and draw lines bisecting the square in both directions (all these lines should intersect at a point at the very center of the square).

2   Place the compass at this center point to draw a 5½-inch-diameter circle, then a 16½-inch-diameter circle, and a 22-inch-diameter circle.

3   Bisect each arc segment of the outer circle and draw connecting lines.

4   Cut out the star shape as well as the center opening with the jigsaw (see Materials and Tools, page 148).

5   Using the wood star as a pattern, draw two star shapes on the felt. Add a 1-inch seam allowance around the outer edge of one star shape. Cut out both star shapes.

6   Glue a layer of fiberfill to one side of the wood star; cut excess away from the edges where necessary.

7   Position the larger felt star on a flat surface; center the wood star (fiberfill side down) on it.

8   Clipping corners and star tips where necessary, pull the outer seam allowance up and glue to the wood back.

9   Using the wood inner circle as a guide, make a series of even snips along the felt inner circle. Turn and glue the resulting tabs to the wood back.

10   Glue the remaining felt shape to the back of the star.

SIZE
Approximately 22" diameter

BASE
22"-diameter plywood star, covered with green felt

MATERIALS AND TOOLS
Plywood, 2' square, ½" thick
1 yard dark green felt, 45" wide
Rhinestone jewelry, such as from flea markets or yard sales, intact or broken
5 yards strung pearls
24 pearl beads
8 hatpins with pearl ends
Bag of polyester fiberfill
Tacky glue
Ruler
Compass
Pencil
Scissors
Drill
Jigsaw

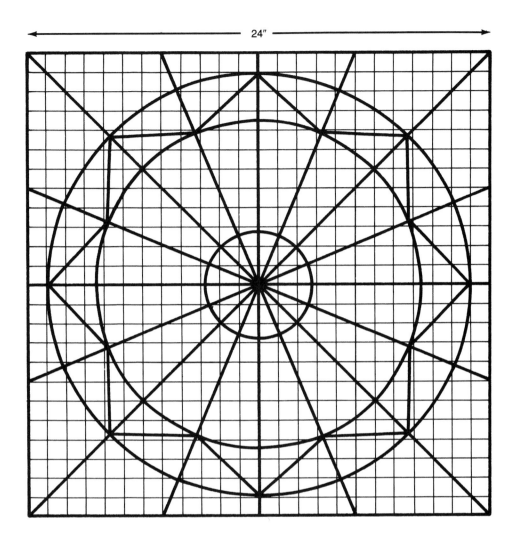

11 Attach a hanger to the base (see How to Hang Your Wreath, page 149).

12 Follow the photograph to glue the strung pearls along the inner and outer edges and to define the separations.

13 Remove backs from the rhinestone jewelry pieces so they lie flat. Arrange jewelry on the star, using broken pieces to fill in small areas, and hot-glue each piece one by one.

14 Slip three pearls onto each hatpin; put a little glue on the pin tips and push one into each star point.

JOY TO THE WORLD

Call up both the sounds and the colors of the holiday season with a wreath like this one, which the designer originally entitled Musicalia.

Louise Lorentzen of Greenwood, Virginia

In 1980 Louise Lorentzen was a single parent in graduate school, with three teenage children at home and no budget for Christmas presents. So she made wreaths from the boxwood growing on her property in rural Virginia.

These gifts stimulated requests for "such beautiful wreaths," and this, says Louise, "set my business instincts in motion." For the following seven years she made and sold boxwood wreaths every holiday season.

Five years ago she realized she couldn't make enough live boxwood wreaths to meet the seasonal demand, so she turned to grapevine wreaths, using material from a nearby vineyard. Again the demand was too great to fill during the short season.

So she searched for sources of artificial greenery and at last, in 1989, was able to make more than one hundred wreaths while also working as a research scientist/sociologist at the University of Virginia School of Nursing. At the end of that hectic year she resigned from academia to devote herself full-time to her wreath business.

TO MAKE THE WREATH

1 Attach a hanger to the base (see How to Hang Your Wreath, page 149).

2 With 74 inches of the red flocked ribbon form a bow with six 6-inch loops. (Follow the French bow instructions in How to Form Bows, page 154. However, wire the bow together after Step 4 has been completed, and omit remaining steps.) Cut two 15-inch flocked streamers.

3 Hot-glue the flocked ribbon bow to the wreath, as shown in the photograph.

4 Glue the ends of the flocked ribbon streamers to the center of the bow. Ripple the streamers and glue them to the wreath to hold. Notch ends.

5 With 26 inches of the kraft-paper ribbon, form and wire together a bow with two 6-inch loops. Cut four streamers: two 11½ inches long and two 13½ inches long.

6 Ripple the 13½-inch-long kraft-paper ribbon streamers to follow the contours of the flocked ribbon streamers, as shown in the photograph. Glue the ends to the center of the bow and glue the kraft-paper streamers to the flocked streamers.

7 Glue the kraft-paper ribbon bow on top of the flocked bow, covering the top of the streamers.

8 Following the photograph, slip an end of each 11½-inch-long streamer under each side of the flocked bow. Ripple and swirl them; glue in place. Notch ends of all the kraft-paper streamers.

SIZE
Approximately 18" diameter

BASE
18"-diameter artificial pine wreath

MATERIALS AND TOOLS
3 yards red flocked ribbon, 2½" wide
2¼ yards wire-edge kraft-paper ribbon printed with Christmas music, 2½" wide
26 baby's breath clusters
6 gilded pinecones
3 gilded crabapples, 1½" wide
4 clusters of ½"-diameter red berries with leaves
Floral wire
Wire cutters
Scissors
Glue gun

9 Arrange the pinecones, crabapples, and berry and leaf clusters; glue.

10 Tuck small clusters of baby's breath into the wreath. Apply a small dot of glue to each stem, to hold in place.

Designer's Note

For Louise Lorentzen a new wreath design begins with the bow: "It defines the wreath." After attaching the bow she generally glues the streamers in place, effecting a rippling look. Once the bow and streamers are attached she lays out the rest of the wreath except for the baby's breath. This way she can choose, reject, or move items around to achieve the right look. She then glues each item on one by one.

Inserting the baby's breath is always her last step. The clusters of tiny flowers not only act as a pleasing accent but cover flaws and integrate the design.

GENERAL
DIRECTIONS

WREATH BASES

Although a wreath base often ends up being covered, it should always be appropriate to the finished project. Consider the kinds of materials being used, how heavy they are, and how they will be attached. Also focus on the wreath's color, size, and shape, and whether the base will show when your wreath is completed.

Choices of wreath bases are wide and varied. Available are straw, excelsior, plastic foam, wire frames, and naturals such as vines, willow, or twigs.

These all come in a wide range of sizes and shapes. Some can be as small as 3 inches in diameter or as wide as 24 inches—or even larger. Most are circular, but some are oval or even heart-shaped.

Straw

Straw held onto a wire frame by nylon line makes a very compact, versatile wreath. It often comes wrapped in plastic, which can be removed easily and most frequently should be removed. Sometimes, however, the plastic can be left on to strengthen the construction of the wreath, depending on the materials and coverage needed.

Straw is attractive enough to be left exposed, so that it becomes part of the wreath design. It's available in rounds of different sizes and sometimes as an oval. Materials can be attached with liquid glue, hot-glue gun, U-pins, picks, or wire.

Excelsior

Formed from tightly packed excelsior, or excelsior around a straw core, this type of base comes in colors and in heart shapes, as well as in rounds. Handle an excelsior wreath as you would a straw one.

Plastic Foam

Green or white plastic-foam rings or hearts come with straight or curved sides and are sometimes reinforced by a core wire for heavier projects. They look better when covered totally with materials that can be attached with U-pins or floral picks (use a touch of glue on their points to hold them permanently), a cool-melt glue gun, or liquid glue.

Wire Frames

Wire frames are available in several sizes, as a single wire to which materials like Spanish moss or artificial pine are wired, or as a dimensional double frame that can contain in its well added moss or rounds of vines secured by wire wound around the frame. Additional trim and materials can be put on with liquid glue or a hot-glue gun.

Naturals

The most common natural base is grapevine. These wreaths are available as small as 3 inches in diameter and can be found as wide as 2 feet or more. Because vines shape well, bases made of them can be found shaped as hearts and ovals as well as rounds, in natural, bleached, or colored finishes. Willow, which is heavier and smoother than grapevine, is usually bleached but may also be tinted in soft colors. Left partially exposed, these natural materials can become part of the wreath's overall design. All methods of attachment can be used: liquid glue, hot-glue gun, wire, and picks.

MATERIALS AND TOOLS

To help in harvesting the naturals needed, as well as in constructing the wreath itself, a wreath-maker might invest in some basic tools.

Cutters

Good quality cutting tools, ones that are strong and sharp, can reduce the time and effort required to make a wreath and help produce designs with a professional look. To be kept in working order, these tools should be used only for what they were designed: scissors for ribbon or fabric, wire cutters for wire. If you abide by this rule, your tools will last a long time and prove to be a worthwhile investment.

Pruning shears are handy for cutting vines or light branches.

Garden shears can lop off flower heads, stems, or leaves very quickly.

Wire cutters for snipping floral wire should also be strong enough to cut through heavier wire, such as clothes-hanger wire.

Scissors should be the sharpest available for cutting fabric or ribbon. Have a second pair for cutting paper and other materials.

Utility knives with changeable blades are always handy for cutting through cardboard or foamcore.

Serrated knives are best for slicing through plastic foam blocks or sheets.

A jigsaw offers the quickest and easiest way to cut a ring or heart shape out of wood. If a center opening is to be cut, first drill a hole in that area. Stick the blade of the jigsaw into the resulting hole and cut out the opening.

Aids for Easy Handling

The wreath-making process requires tools to hold materials in place while hot glue is applied or to handle items too small to be easily positioned with the fingers.

Needlenose pliers are useful in twisting wire to make wreath hangers or holding material on the wreath. They can also help to bend and shape wire to form a wreath base.

Tweezers work perfectly for handling or holding small materials in place, such as shells, pinecones, or baby roses.

Fasteners

Fasteners are critical in attaching decorative elements to practically any type of base.

Wires come in various gauges. The thinner the wire, the higher its gauge number. Wire is used to attach bows or other materials and to hang wreaths. It is also a material from which wreath bases or hangers may be made.

U-pins, somewhat like hairpins, have two sharp points that can fix an object such as a flower to a wreath base. They work well on plastic foam, straw, or excelsior bases.

Picks are small wood sticks with a point at one end and, at the other, wires that can be wound around a flower or other object. So a pick with the point poked into plastic foam or straw provides a very firm hold.

Floral tape in a choice of colors is handy for securing materials and for camouflaging wires.

Finally, if the materials or bows are not wired to the wreath, then a glue gun or a bottle or tube of tacky glue is essential to doing a permanent job of holding things together.

The glue gun is probably the most important tool wreath-designers use. Although thumb-feed glue guns are available, the easiest gun to work with is one with a trigger that ensures a steady flow of glue. Also available are a glue gun that provides twelve minutes of cord-free gluing in case an electric outlet is not nearby, and a low-temperature glue gun that works well on delicate synthetic materials and on items such as balloons, plastic foam, or dried flowers. All of these guns are made in different sizes and use glue sticks that come in a variety of formulas for different gluing tasks.

Tacky glue is a thick, white liquid glue that stays put while drying, has good adhering qualities, and dries quickly.

HOW TO HANG YOUR WREATH

"A hanger on the back of the wreath assures its staying firmly hung and that it will be displayed as it was meant to be," explains wreath-designer Susie Light.

No matter what the base is, don't hang the wreath itself over a hook or nail without an appropriate fastener or hanger on the back. This enables the wreath to rest firmly on its nail or hook.

The appropriate type of hanger is dictated by the base used and the weight of the finished wreath. Attaching a hanger often requires handling the wreath roughly, so remember to put it on before fragile material is attached. Also, when you put a hanger on in an early stage, it can more readily be hidden by a bow or other materials.

All-Purpose Hanger

A good all-purpose hanger can be made from a 6-inch piece of stiff wire formed into an inverted U. A clothes hanger is perfect because it already has curves at its outer ends. Using needlenose pliers, bend the lower 1½ inches of both ends up at right angles to the inverted U. To attach the hanger, run wire or tape over the angled ends and around the plastic foam, straw, vine, or wire wreath (see diagram).

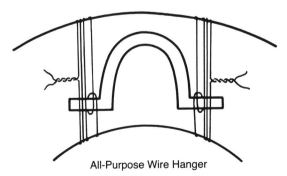

All-Purpose Wire Hanger

Plastic-Foam Base

If the wreath will be heavy, reinforce the area where the hanger will be placed by first wrapping it with a couple of rounds of masking or duct tape. This will prevent any wire wrapped around the wreath from chewing through the foam.

Next, wind floral wire around the tape a couple of times and form a ring on the back by twisting the wire, or twist on a small plastic or metal curtain ring to act as a hanger, or use the all-purpose hanger.

Wood Base

Because wood bases are usually made from thin wood, the hanger must be attached with very short nails or screws if they are not to show through the front of the wreath. This is not a problem when the front of the base is being covered with material. Available are sawtooth picture hangers using tiny nails, picture frame hangers that can be tapped in, and picture hangers with adhesive backs.

Another solution is to screw a pair of ½-inch screw eyes into the upper back of the base about 2 to 3 inches apart, and stretch picture wire between them to hang over a nail or hook on the wall. To keep the wreath from tipping back at the bottom while it's hanging, center a third screw eye at the bottom back of the base.

Wreath designer Indy Bacon solved the problem of determining the top of her ring of driftwood Twinkling Santas (page 79) by evenly spacing seven screw eyes around the back with picture wire stretched through them. Thus, family members who worked on the wreath can move it around from time to time to position someone's favorite Santa right on top.

Straw Base

If the front and sides of the base will be covered with material, wrap wire around it first and form a ring on the back, or attach a small plastic or metal curtain ring with a twist of wire, or use the all-purpose hanger.

If the base is not to be covered, as in the Chili Lights wreath of Susan Wilson (page 18), work a stiff wire through the upper back of the wreath and form a ring out of it.

Cardboard Base

A picture hanger with an adhesive back works best. If the front of the base will be covered with material, wrap wire around it first and form a ring on the back, or attach a small plastic or metal curtain ring with a twist of wire, or use the all-purpose hanger.

Vine and Wire Bases

These can be wrapped with wire and a ring formed on the back, or use the all-purpose hanger. Or, for a hanger that's not visible from the front, stretch a short piece of picture wire across the upper back of the wreath and twist it to hold on the wire base or vines.

ABOUT RIBBONS AND BOWS

Nearly half of our wreaths are accented by bows. Bows often act as the final finishing touch to a wreath, the element that ties the wreath together, although some designers let the bow and its ribbon dictate how the rest of the wreath is going to look.

Bows depend on the materials used: Their final shape and size are often determined by the quality and other characteristics of the ribbon, whether it is a woven type (such as satin, taffeta, or velvet) or paper, lace, tulle, net, or materials such as raffia, cording, or yarn. Ribbon can be as narrow as 1/16 inch and as wide as 4 inches—with 6-inch widths for tulle or net.

Ribbons can be found in fabric and sewing supply stores, crafts supply shops, nursery and garden supply stores, variety stores, and even at florists' shops.

Starting with the most important tool, sharp scissors, to prevent fraying while cutting, try making the same bow with different ribbon widths and different numbers of loops to see how the bow changes. Try layering a plaid bow on top of a flocked one, as Susie Light did on her Jolly Snowmen and Friends wreath (page 69).

Form the same bow with different materials. Experiment with satins, taffetas, moirés, lace, grosgrains, velvets, sheers, foils, Lurex, and metallics for shine and craft ribbons printed with everything from florals to fish, from dots to ducks.

Wire-edge taffeta, Lurex, printed cotton, and sheer ribbons come in several widths and are the ultimate for making a lush bow with

undulating streamers. The effect is stunning, with not too much effort required. Charlene Geiger added her own special touch to her In Love with Another Era wreath (page 116) by using a hair crimper on her wire-edge ribbon bow and streamers.

Reaching beyond the fabric ribbons we are all familiar with, we find tulle on Jeanne Brackin's Nostalgia in Tulle wreath (page 120), strands of raffia on Kathy Zawacki's Vegetable Fantasy wreath (page 59), and paper twist forming an elaborate bow with streamers on Pam Hoover's Autumn Harvest wreath (page 54).

Curling ribbon adds a festive touch to Kay Dugger's Balloons for Birthdays wreath (page 72), and an orange open-weave ribbon bow is perfect for Susan Sanville's spooky Boo! It's Halloween wreath (page 66).

Ribbons to Suit the Bow Design

Working with different ribbons makes us familiar with their limitations. Craft ribbon, for example, is available in a wide variety of widths, patterns, and colors, but it is also stiff and unyielding and thus difficult to form into an attractive bow. If it is used, the loops should be wired together with the streamers attached, instead of tied into a bow.

Many of the wreaths in the book have ribbons swirling around them. Ribbons used for such designs should be soft and drapey so they can undulate easily. Narrow to medium widths of satin, taffeta, moiré, and lace work well.

Smart Buying

Bows and swirling ribbons use up a lot of yardage. Costs sometimes can be reduced by purchasing ribbon by the roll rather than by the yard. If many yards of a solid color are needed, acetate satin ribbon might be considered, because it tends to be less expensive than other, fancier ribbons and comes in a wide range of colors and widths.

Polyester seam binding and lace hem facing and seam binding are available in a wide range of colors and are a good value, although limited in widths and yardage.

Ribbons never go out of style and can be a bargain besides. Old woven ribbons such as satins, taffetas, jacquards, or other unusual types can be found at flea markets, second-hand or antique stores, and incorporated into a wreath the way LoRae Pursian did with her Great-Grandma wreath (page 114).

To Freshen Old or Antique Ribbons

Consider old or previously used ribbon even if it is slightly soiled, because it sometimes can be washed in gentle suds and cool water (test-wash a scrap first). Afterward, rinse well, run the ribbon between two fingers to squeeze out the excess water, and hang it up to dry. This can be tried with many types of woven ribbons, but not with velvet.

A lukewarm iron will get rid of wrinkles, but test first. To freshen up a wrinkled ribbon already made into a bow, a shot of steam from an iron held away from the bow is often enough. Most ribbons cannot take too much heat or moisture.

To prevent stored ribbons from wrinkling or being crushed, keep them on their original rolls. Or wind leftover pieces around pieces of stiff cardboard. Hold the starting end in place with tape and the outside end with a small straight pin or a paper clip. Small rolls and wound pieces can be stored in shoe boxes for easy access.

Finally, what to do with short ends of ribbon left over from several projects? Jill M. Oleksy's Just Ribbons wreath (page 138) offers a good way to utilize such small scraps: Just make the same wreath with multicolored ribbons. Or if you have a range of pastels or brights, simply tuck them in here and there, as Nancy F. Smith did with her Lacy Sentiment wreath (page 122).

HOW TO FORM BOWS

Although working with ribbon can seem daunting at first, our tips and a little practice will make the forming of any one of our bows a good deal easier.

Some Tips for Bow-making

To make handling the ribbons easier: When making bows, often one or both hands are involved in manipulating the ribbon, so it's very helpful to have all tools and materials within easy reach and ready to use.

Set out sharp scissors and lengths of wire already cut to wrap around the formed bow.

If streamers are being wired on, complete the bow first, wiring the loops together to hold until the streamers go on—before attaching the bow to the wreath.

To figure a bow's width: Whenever a bow is shown on one of our wreaths, its individual instructions will specify the measurement of the bow's loop. When they specify a 5-inch-wide loop, this means that the loop measures 5 inches from its center to its outer edges.

To form a ribbon round: A round of ribbon is sometimes specified to finish a bow. (Actually, it often is a way to hide the wire holding the bow together.) Measure ribbon to the length specified; add 1 inch for overlap. Cut, wrap, and twist a wire where the ribbon overlaps. Use the wire ends to attach the ribbon round to the bow.

Decorative treatments for streamers: The ends of ribbon streamers can be finished decoratively by cutting notches into them or by cutting them on the diagonal. They can also be pinked with pinking shears, and some ribbons, such as satin, can be fringed by pulling out a number of threads running across the ribbon.

To make bows on your own: The instructions for each wreath in the book specify the amount of ribbon needed to produce the bow that graces that particular wreath.

To estimate the ribbon length needed to make a bow on your own, you need to know the width of each loop (multiplied by 2, for upper and lower parts), the number of loops, and the length and number of streamers needed. The following formula can help:

Width of each loop × 2 × number of loops + (number of streamers × their length) = length of ribbon needed for most bows. Add 3 inches in the case of a French bow, unless otherwise specified, to start the initial roll.

Of course, if you plan to use a ribbon round, add that measurement, plus overlap, to your total.

Bow Shapes

The wreaths shown in this book feature four basic bow shapes.

Two-Loop Bow: The two-loop bow is the type we all know, the one we learned when we were taught to tie our shoes. This bow is seen on Kathy Zawacki's Vegetable Fantasy wreath (page 59) made from multi-strands of raffia. It's also used to attach Carol R. Braverman's From Us in the U.S.A. wreath to its backing ring (page 95) and used over and over again buried in tulle in Jeanne Brackin's Nostalgia in Tulle wreath (page 120).

To Form a Two-Loop Bow

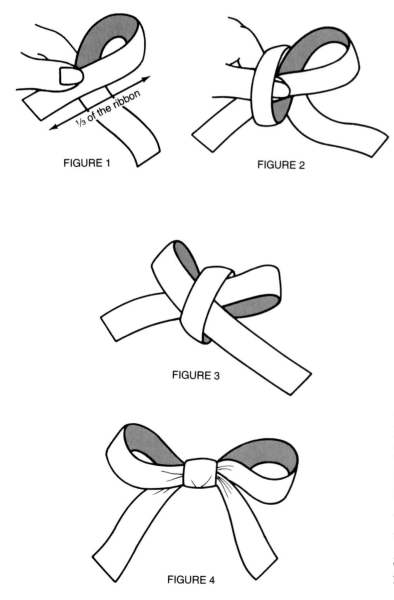

FIGURE 1

FIGURE 2

FIGURE 3

FIGURE 4

1. About one-third of the way into the ribbon with which you're working, form a loop as wide as needed. Hold it in place with the thumb and index fingers of the left hand.

2. Flip the right tail from Figure 1 up and over the left thumb and around to the back of the loop.

3. Form a loop from the right tail in Figure 2; insert it through the loop around the left thumb.

4. Pull the loop up and tighten it. At the same time, adjust both loops and streamers so they are of even lengths.

Starburst Bow: The next shape is the starburst bow, a group of loops radiating from a central point, such as the lace and ribbon combination on Patrice Scholtes-Hightower's Victorian Grace wreath (page 126) or the plaid bow layered on top of a flocked bow in Susie Light's Jolly Snowmen and Friends wreath (page 69).

To Form a Starburst Bow
(See diagrams at right.)

1. From the ribbon length specified, make a ring. To figure its diameter, double the measurement of the loops that are needed. Tape the ribbon end to the inside of the ring.

2. Hold the ribbon ring in one hand and with the other hand roll on enough ribbon layers to make the number of loops needed.

3. Press the ring together in the middle.

4. Fold the flattened ring in half. Using a very sharp scissors, held diagonally, clip off both corners of the folded end.

5. Open out the flattened ring and twist floral wire around the matched center, leaving two long ends with which to attach the bow (unless you plan to hot-glue it in place).

6. Using the right index finger, pull out a loop from inside the bow.

7. Bring the loop down and across the bow with a sharp twist, so it will hold its position.

8. With the left index finger, pull the next loop from the center and twist it down again.

9. Repeat these steps until all the loops are pulled out and twisted into a radiating position.

10. Use the hanging wires or hot glue to attach the bow to the wreath.

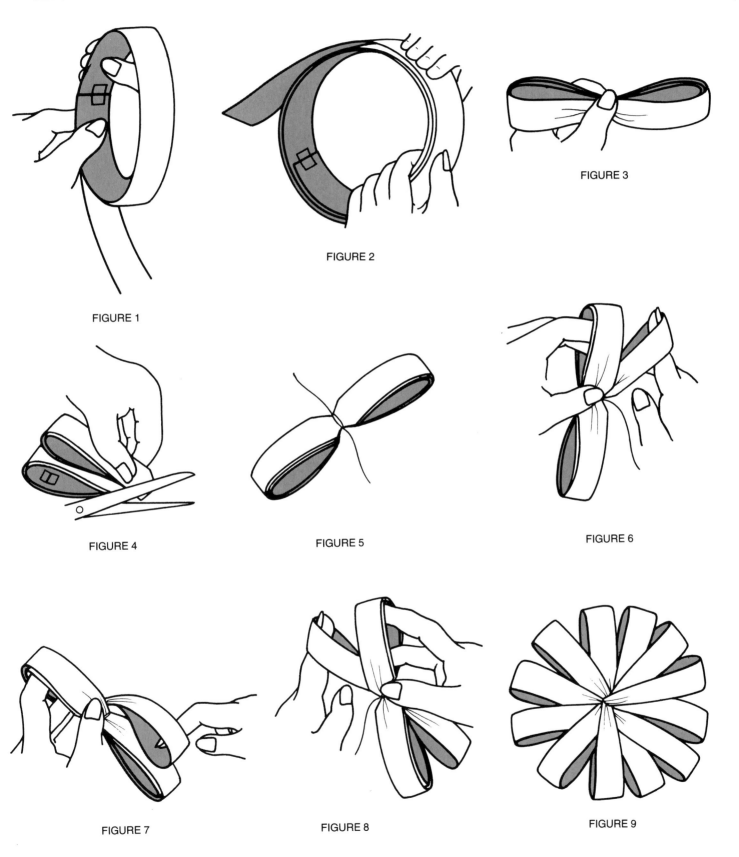

FIGURE 1

FIGURE 2

FIGURE 3

FIGURE 4

FIGURE 5

FIGURE 6

FIGURE 7

FIGURE 8

FIGURE 9

Florist's Bow: The third type is the puffy florist's bow. Maurice A. Parkonen, Jr.'s Cranberry Jewel wreath (page 30) is accented with such a bow executed in flocked ribbon. Although flocked ribbon tends to be stiff, this bow works well because of its large scale. The florist's bow shows up again, in lace, on Yvonne H. Childs' Piggie Heaven wreath (page 15) and yet again in moiré on Connie Boyett's Best Wishes wreath (page 92).

To Form a Florist's Bow

1. Holding the ribbon in the left hand, form a loop as wide as needed. Pinch the bottom of the loop between the thumb and index fingers to create the center of the bow.

2. Twist the long length of ribbon at the pinch and form another loop the same width as the first. Bring this ribbon up to the center and pinch it tightly.

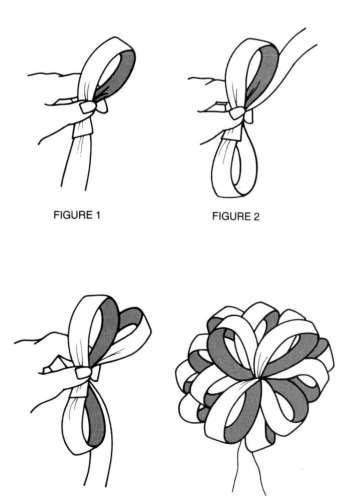

FIGURE 1   FIGURE 2

FIGURE 3   FIGURE 4

3. Again twist the long ribbon end and form another loop the same as the other two. Continue twisting the ribbon, forming a loop and then pinching it in at the center until the ribbon is used up.

4. Continuing to hold all the pinched loops in place, twist and tie a piece of floral wire around the center of the bow, leaving, if desired, two long ends to attach it later (or use hot glue).

French Bow: The last shape is the French bow, a softly elegant one that can be varied simply by adding more loops to the steps shown in the instructions. The French bow is formed in lace on Ruth W. Ratcliff's Beads, Buttons, and Bows wreath (page 106) and with paper twist on the Autumn Harvest wreath from Pam Hoover (page 54). It can be layered on top of a two-loop bow like Judie L. Bennett's plaid bows on her Apples at the Hearth wreath (page 132).

To Form a French Bow
(See diagrams at right.)

1. Working with the amount of ribbon specified, roll one end of the ribbon around the left thumb.

2. From the long length of ribbon, form a loop as wide as needed; hold it together with the thumb and index finger.

3. Form the ribbon length into a second loop the same width as the first.

4. Follow Figures 2 and 3 to form two more pairs of loops, placing them diagonally to the first pair.

5. Bring the remaining ribbon end up, around, and under the center of the ring formed in Figure 1. Wrap a length of floral wire around the ring and the ribbon end; twist and tie it, leaving, if desired, two long wire ends with which to attach the bow later.

6. Cut the loop formed by the ribbon end in half for two streamers, and, if desired, notch the ends. Use the two long wire ends to attach the bow or use a hot-glue gun.

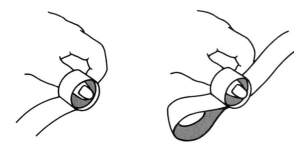

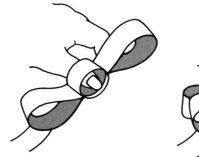

FIGURE 1   FIGURE 2

FIGURE 3   FIGURE 4

FIGURE 5

FIGURE 6

HOW TO DESIGN HEART SHAPES

1 Referring to the width and height given in the individual wreath instructions, mark a square or rectangle on a piece of stiff paper and cut out.

2 Fold and crease the paper in half along its width.

3 Draw a half-heart to completely fill the width and height of the folded paper, using the crease as the vertical center of the heart.

4 Holding the folded sheet of paper closed, cut out the heart pattern through both layers. Unfold the completed heart.

5 Place this heart pattern on the material from which the final heart will be cut, and draw around it.

PROTECTING AND CLEANING YOUR WREATH

These tips for protecting and caring for your wreath come from our designers, many of whom discovered through experience the best ways to give their own wreaths a longer life.

1 Sometimes the care begins while the wreath is being made. Ribbons and fabrics can be sprayed with Scotch-gard Fabric Protector before being attached to a wreath with other materials. If the wreath is all fabric like Jacqueline Misek's Round of Oak Leaves (page 56) or all ribbons like Jill M. Oleksy's Just Ribbons wreath (page 138), the wreath itself can be given a couple of light coats of Scotch-gard Fabric Protector.

2 If bows or artificial silk flowers are likely to get soiled or bedraggled, simply wire them on rather than gluing them, so they can be replaced easily with fresh ones later.

3 Some of our wreath designers use their vacuum cleaners, in reverse, to blow dust away. But before doing this, check that all materials are firmly attached to their base. Give the wreath a shake, and if elements are loose, apply the glue gun or add some extra wire to hold.

4 Designer Liz Reilly has found that a gentle

answer to dusting her flower wreaths is a hair dryer on low heat.

5 Using a spray can that emits air (obtainable from photo and computer supply stores), as Susie Light and Nancy Smith do, helps to blow dust from the hard-to-reach crevices of a wreath.

6 For the lightest touch, use an artist's brush, as Kathryn D. Fix does to dust her dried flower wreath.

7 Silks Alive spray, found in florists' supply stores, is promoted as keeping artificial silk flowers and foliage fresh and clean without wiping.

8 Keep shell and pinecone wreaths clean by wiping them off with a damp cloth.

9 To retain the colors of dried flowers for a longer time, keep the wreath out of the direct rays of the sun.

10 Do not plan to hang a wreath outdoors unless it is weatherproof. Try hanging it on an inside door instead.

STORING AND SHIPPING YOUR WREATH

Storing

The very best storage for any kind of wreath is a cardboard box or a paper bag in preference to a plastic bag, because the paper "breathes" and doesn't hold moisture. Loosely wrap the wreath in tissue paper before boxing or bagging it.

Wreaths that aren't made from natural materials can be stored in plastic bags, but be aware that condensation is always possible, and this may cause some materials to spoil.

To preserve bows when storing or shipping, stuff each loop with a roll of tissue paper, facial tissue, or aluminum foil.

Mice and some insects love dried flowers and foliage. Store wreaths where these pests cannot get at them. Sometimes a handful of mothballs dropped into the bottom of the storage box or into the bagged wreath can act as a deterrent.

If a dried flower wreath is being stored dur-ing humid weather, try hanging small bags of silica gel nearby to reduce the moisture in the area.

Shipping

If a wreath is to travel by mail and arrive in good shape, it must be prevented from shifting in its carton and protected from anything on top that might crush it.

The shipping box should be slightly larger all around than the wreath. Cut a piece of corrugated cardboard (or foamcore) about 2 inches smaller than the bottom of the box.

Place the cardboard on a flat work surface and center the wreath on top of it. Use a pencil to mark four to six evenly spaced pairs of dots around the wreath on the cardboard, one along the inner curve and the other opposite the first, along the outer curve. Remove the wreath temporarily and with an awl or skewer poke holes through the cardboard at the marked dots.

Cut a 2-foot length of wire for each pair of holes. Working through the cardboard from back to front, thread a wire through each pair of holes, one wire end per hole, so that the center of the wire lies flat against the back of the cardboard and the ends extend equally in front.

Replace the wreath on the cardboard and twist pairs of wire ends together above the wreath to hold it in place on the cardboard. If the wreath is particularly fragile, tuck a piece of tissue under each piece of twisted wire to cushion it.

Run strips of double-faced tape along the bottom of the carton and place the wreath and cardboard on top. Place a block of plastic foam the height of the box in the center opening of the wreath and double-face tape it to the bottom of the box. This will prevent the lid of the box from pressing on the wreath.

Gently fill the box with fresh popcorn, recycled foam peanuts, or lightly crushed tissue paper.

Close and tape the lid, mark the box to show which end is up, and your wreath is ready to be shipped.

YOUR WORK SPACE

Although many of our wreath-makers design on a kitchen table, a space that allows for material to be spread around works much better. A simple worktable can be made from a piece of plywood and a pair of folding sawhorses.

Some wreath-making is done on a flat surface, but for checking the progress of the work, hanging the wreath on a wall can be essential. A pegboard wall is ideal for hanging completed wreaths or ones in progress, as well as for storing certain tools.

Important to the work area is a nearby outlet for the glue gun, clamp-on lights, or table lamp to be plugged into.

If the wreath-making is ongoing and materials accumulate, good storage may be provided by open shelves of wood or metal, either permanent or knockdown.

For nonnatural materials and certain tools, plastic boxes make ideal storage containers. Cardboard hat- and shoe-boxes are perfect for holding naturals. Label everything and stack the boxes on the shelves for easy access.

The final essential for easy wreath-making is adequate lighting. Inexpensive lamps with aluminum shades (found in hardware stores) can be clamped onto the edge of the worktable or angled toward the wall area where the work is hung. Table lamps that swivel and move so the work is properly lighted are also useful and widely available.

HOW TO DRY FLOWERS AND OTHER NATURALS

Preserving flowers begins with gathering them. Wreath-designer Deborah DeRosa suggests harvesting them at the various stages of their development: in the bud, in bloom, and, with some, when they're about to set seed.

Pick flowers with lush petals, such as roses or peonies, before their prime so their petals won't shed as they dry.

The object of drying flowers is to get rid of the moisture that causes rotting and mold. A good rule to follow is to start with a dry unblemished flower picked just before its peak, because damaged or aging flowers will not be improved by the drying process.

Flowers and other naturals should be gathered only in dry weather, in the afternoon or evening before sunset, when the dew has fully evaporated and naturals are at their driest. Certainly never gather them right after a rain.

When flowers will be used in a wreath, it is not necessary to cut them with long stems, but with just enough stem to make them easy to handle.

Drying Conditions

Ideally, flowers should be air-dried in a darkened room to help preserve their color. The area should also be dry and well ventilated to allow air to circulate around the plant material and so prevent mold and rotting. An uninsulated, hot, dry attic is a perfect environment for drawing moisture out of flowers.

Drying times depend on the individual flowers, the conditions under which they are picked, and where and how they are dried. Drying time can range from two days for silica-dried material to a month or so for air-drying. Check on the state of the flowers every couple of days to prevent overdrying—when flowers are dried too long, they may disintegrate when handled.

Air-Drying: Air-drying is the most common simple drying method.

Strip the flowers of their leaves immediately after picking them, and wipe their stems dry of any moisture. Gather them into bunches of four to six stems of the same type of flower so they will all dry in the same amount of time. Join the bunches with a very tight rubber band that will contract as the flower stems dry and shrink up. Wind a string around the stems, so the flower bunch can be hung upside down from a nail on a beam or from a clothesline strung across an open area. (Use clothespins to attach the string.) Keeping the flower heads down allows them to dry straight.

Check the drying process every so often and, if necessary, rearrange the stems within a bunch, or even the bunches themselves, to be certain they are all receiving the same amount of circulated dry air.

As soon as the flowers are dry, remove them from the drying area, because if flowers dry too long they will disintegrate with handling.

The Silica-Gel Method: The silica-gel method requires less drying time but is a more expensive method than air-drying.

Silica gel is excellent for retaining the color and shape of flowers, but don't use this method if the climate is humid or the wreath is to be hung in a damp bathroom or kitchen, because silica-gel-treated flowers tend to reabsorb moisture more readily.

Silica gel crystals, noted for their moisture-absorbing properties, are sold at florists' supply stores and pharmacies. The crystals should have the texture of fine coffee grounds. If they don't, this texture can be achieved by running them through a food processor or blender.

A large round cookie tin or a shallow plastic storage container with a lid works well for drying with silica gel. Cover the bottom of the container with the crystals to a depth of about 1 inch.

Cut off almost the entire stem of each flower to be dried, but leave a short length for handling. Place the flower head on top of the silica, facing down. With the use of a small spoon or scoop, gently cover the flower head with the silica, making certain that crystals fill the crevices between the petals. (This is why the crystals must be so fine: so they don't crush and distort the flower.) Put in as many flowers as can fit in the container without touching each other. Cover the container.

After a couple of days examine the flowers. If the petals are like dry paper, they are ready. If not, return them to dry a little longer. Don't overdry them, or the petals will become too brittle and fragile to handle.

When the flowers have dried satisfactorily, use a slotted spoon to remove them one at a time from the container. While the flower is on the spoon, use an artist's brush to brush away any excess silica crystals.

The crystals can then be dried out in a low oven and used again to dry flowers.

Storing Dried Flowers

Once the flowers are dried they must be stored in a cool, dry, airy place; otherwise they will become limp and wilted.

They can be packed in cardboard boxes (shoe boxes are ideal) with tissue or newspaper placed loosely around them. Leave the box uncovered so air can reach the blossoms. If silica-gel-dried flowers are being stored, sprinkle some of the crystals on the bottom of the box to prevent moisture from being picked up by the flowers.

Do not use plastic for wrapping the flowers, because it retains moisture and can ruin the dried flowers.

INDEX

All of us at Meredith® Press are dedicated to offering you, our customer, the best books we can create. We are particularly concerned that all of the instructions for making projects are clear and accurate. Please address your correspondence to: Customer Service Department, Meredith® Press, Meredith Corporation, 150 East 52nd Street, New York, NY 10022; or call 1-800-678-2665.